Defending Mexican Valor in Texas

José Antonio Navarro
This is an undated, enlarged depiction from an original photograph.
Courtesy Casa Navarro State Historical Park, San Antonio.

Defending Mexican Valor in Texas

José Antonio Navarro's Historical Writings,
1853-1857

José Antonio Navarro

edited by
David R. McDonald
and
Timothy M. Matovina

STATE HOUSE PRESS
Austin, Texas
1995

Library of Congress Cataloging-in-Publication Data

Navarro, José Antonio, 1795-1871.
[Apuntes históricos interesantes de San Antonio de Béxar. English & Spanish]
Defending Mexican valor in Texas : José Antonio Navarro's historical
writings, 1853-1857 / José Antonio Navarro ; edited by David R. McDonald
and Timothy M. Matovina.
p. cm.
Includes bibliographical references and index.
ISBN 1-880510-31-6 (alk. paper : hardcover).
ISBN 1-880510-32-4 (alk. paper : papercover)
1. Texas—History—Revolution, 1835-1836. 2. Texas—History—Republic,
1836-1846. 3. Navarro, José Antonio, 1795-1871. 4.
Statesmen—Texas—Biography. I. McDonald, David R., 1941- .
II. Matovina, Timothy M., 1955- . III. Title.
F390.N3813 1995
976.4'03'092—dc20   95-38156

Printed in the United States of America

First Edition

Some passages from the introductory essay "José Antonio Navarro: Tejano
Advocate and Historical Chronicler" are based on selections from an earlier
work by Dr. Timothy M. Matovina, *Tejano Religion and Ethnicity: San
Antonio, 1821-1860*. The authors gratefully acknowledge the University of
Texas Press for permission to republish this material.

cover design by David Timmons

STATE HOUSE PRESS
P.O. Box 15247
Austin, Texas 78761

an imperfect but truthful history

> *for the humanitarian and cultured*
> *who understand how to respect*
> *and sympathize with the suffering*
> *of a valiant people*

—José Antonio Navarro

Table of Contents

List Of Illustrations

Preface

While the flags of Spain, Mexico, the Republic of Texas, the United States, and the Confederacy successively flew over San Antonio, many Texans of Mexican or Spanish descent (Tejanos) influenced the momentous events which shaped their history. None played a more important role in the public affairs of Texas than José Antonio Navarro.

In addition to his long and significant political career, Navarro authored the first Tejano publication on Texas history. Entitled *Apuntes históricos interesantes de San Antonio de Béxar* (Commentaries of Historical Interest on San Antonio de Béxar), this important work was first published in English translation as a series of newspaper articles in the 1850s. In 1869, San Antonio merchant Narciso Leal and his friends published a Spanish version as a short book. *Apuntes* has been virtually unavailable to both Spanish and English readers for more than a century; its republication is long overdue and most appropriate in this bicentennial year of Navarro's birth.

The purpose of *Apuntes* was to oppose accounts, common in the English-language press, that scorned Texas' Mexican history and heritage. A native San Antonian, Navarro witnessed the heroism of local Tejanos during the Mexican struggle for independence from Spain. In *Apuntes* he recounted this heroism to counter histories written by Anglo Americans—

new Texans who disregarded the Tejano legacy which preceded them.

Besides taking a stand against biased Anglo-American historical accounts, Navarro's *Apuntes* is also a valuable source for local events during the Mexican War of Independence. A perceptive eyewitness, Navarro's vivid narrative engages the imagination as well as the intellect. For example, he provides a striking portrayal of Juan Bautista Casas and Juan Manuel Zambrano, two major figures of the insurgency and counter-revolution at San Antonio de Béxar. Although he erred in a few minor details as he wrote his commentaries four decades after the events described, his account relates dramatic encounters of people caught in a violent conflict that produced intense emotions of hope, fear, hatred, agony and horror. Apuntes accomplished Navarro's original intention of promoting respect for Tejanos by chronicling their historical achievements; it also left an evocative historical narrative for posterity.

A somewhat complicated publishing history has created a tangle that needs clarification. The original 1850s Spanish manuscript in Navarro's hand is not extant. Half of the account initially appeared in English translation in the *Western Texan* (San Antonio) of December 1, 1853. A copy of this rare document is in the Lamar papers at the Texas State Archives in Austin and is published in the well-known *The Papers of Mirabeau Buonaparte Lamar*, 4:5-12. Although the editors of the *Western Texan* did not cite an author for this account, it is clearly an English translation of the historical narrative attributed to Navarro in the later 1869 Spanish edition of *Apuntes*. The other half of Navarro's historical commentaries was published in three installments of the *San Antonio Ledger* beginning on December 12, 1857 and ending with the issue of January 2, 1858. In the 1869 Spanish edition, the earlier newspaper installments were rearranged to reflect the historical chronology of the events described. The compilers of that work added the correspondence through which they secured Navarro's permission to print his work in Spanish. They also added a biographical sketch of Navarro, an anonymous reflection on the past and present in San Antonio de Béxar, and two poems about San Antonio by Ponciano B. Fernández. *Apuntes* also states that the *Ledger* installments were partially republished in the *Boletín del Pueblo* (Camargo, Tamaulipas, Mexico) during 1858, but this source has not surfaced. The only further effort to make *Apuntes* accessible in the past 125 years was an unpublished English translation apparently done by Edward S. Sears in the 1930s.

This present volume provides a new and annotated translation of the 1869 Spanish edition, along with a facsimile in the original Spanish. For clarity, Navarro's commentaries are presented in the order in which he wrote them. The biographical sketch of Navarro and aforementioned correspondence are included, but the anonymous reflection on San Antonio de Béxar and the two poems are omitted because they add no further insight into Navarro's historical account. An introductory essay summarizes pertinent elements of Navarro's public career and examines the historical context in which he wrote his *Apuntes*.

We are grateful to all those who enhanced this volume with their expertise. Jack Jackson, Gerald E. Poyo, Dora Guerra, Jesús F. de la Teja, Félix D. Almaráz, Jr., and Chris Megargee offered valuable comments on various parts of the manuscript. Francisca Luna proofread the translation and transcription of *Apuntes*. Issis Vela assisted with archival research in the San Antonio area; Allan F. Jose and H. Joel Schmidt obtained vital information at the Library of Congress in Washington, D.C. Jo Myler, Frank Faulkner, and the staff in the history and reference department of the San Antonio

Public Library have been consistent collaborators for this project, as have the archivists at The Center for American History, University of Texas, Austin. Above all, we thank the Navarro descendants who have encouraged our work and in numerous ways have supported ongoing research about José Antonio Navarro and the Navarro family.

David R. McDonald
Timothy M. Matovina

José Antonio Navarro:

Tejano Advocate
and Historical Chronicler

José Antonio Baldomero Navarro was born in San Antonio de Béxar on February 27, 1795, the son of Angel Navarro, a merchant and native of the island of Corsica, and native San Antonian María Josefa Ruiz y Peña. As a young man Navarro was deeply affected by the dramatic events in his home town during the critical years from 1811 to 1813, when control of San Antonio seesawed between Spanish royalists and Mexican insurgent forces. Public displays of cruel and violent acts on both sides horrified the young Navarro, but he was also inspired by the courageous actions of San Antonians as they fought for independence from Spain. Later he emerged as the premier advocate for Texans of Mexican or Spanish descent (Tejanos) during the turbulent decades when Texas sovereignty passed from Spain, to Mexico, to the Texas Republic, to the United States, to the Confederate States of America, and then back to the United States. In this time of social upheaval Navarro was a unifying figure for a Tejano community which struggled to endure. Although occupied with his profession as a merchant and land investor, he consistently represented his fellow San Antonians in various political bodies under the governments of Mexico, the Republic of Texas, and the United States. He also promoted Tejano interests as a private citizen, remaining influential in public affairs until his death in 1871.

The earliest biographical sketch of Navarro, a brief entry in the 1858 work *Texas: Her Resources and Her Public Men*, labeled him an "Americanized Texian." Writing for a readership in the United States, the author highlighted three activities from Navarro's lengthy political career: his efforts to promote the interests of Anglo-American colonists in the Coahuila y Tejas legislature, his support of Texas independence from Mexico, and his role as commissioner of the Santa Fe expedition, an effort to wrest eastern New Mexico from the Mexican Republic and incorporate it into the newly formed Republic of Texas. Subsequent works have perpetuated this view of Navarro; Joseph Martin Dawson's 1969 biography of Navarro even replaces the "Americanized Texian" label with that of "Anglocized Mexican."[1]

Narciso Leal and his companions' 1869 biographical sketch depicts Navarro in an entirely different light. While confirming that Navarro supported Texas independence from the Mexican dictator Antonio López de Santa Anna, Leal and his friends emphasized that after Texas independence Navarro was "the strongest champion of the rights of [his] people."[2] Under the governments of the Texas Republic and the United States, Navarro defended Tejano land claims, suffrage, and citizenship rights. He also spoke out for Tejano interests in open letters, speeches, and letters to newspaper editors. In the 1850s, he authored a version of local history to counteract Anglo-American treatises which ignored, diminished, or incorrectly reported the historical contribution of Tejanos. Drawing on his vivid recollections of Tejano valor during the

Mexican struggle for independence from
tiqued Anglo-American histories which ch
as the victims of a morally and intellect
heritage. First published in the local E
Anglo-American ascendancy to economic and political control of his native San Antonio, Navarro's historical writings
reflect his role as a defender of his people during the transition
from Spanish to U.S. rule.

Navarro and Anglo-American Interests

As noted, most of Navarro's biographers have focused on the
ways his political agenda converged with that of Anglo Americans. For example, they underscore his mutually beneficial
relationship with Stephen F. Austin, the most noteworthy
leader of the early Anglo-American colonization in Texas.
Tejano leaders like Navarro saw increased colonization as
necessary to address the Native-American threat and the economic development of Texas. Since there were few new
arrivals from within the Mexican Republic itself, Anglo-
American immigrants were seen as a needed asset for future
progress in Texas. Thus Navarro and Austin had a vested
interest in legislation which facilitated Anglo-American colonization. In 1828, for instance, the *ayuntamiento* (town council) of Austin's colony at San Felipe sent a proposal to Ramón
Músquiz, the *jefe político* (political chief) at San Antonio de
Béxar and highest ranking Mexican official in Texas at the time.
This proposal was an attempt to circumvent antislavery stat-
utes by legalizing the practice of bringing "servants or hire-
lings" to Texas from "foreign countries." Músquiz directed the
San Felipe proposal to Navarro and Miguel Arciniega, the two
Texas representatives at the state legislature in Saltillo. Navarro
presented the prospective law on the floor of the legislature

nd reported to Austin his "good fortune" in securing its passage. Although such initiatives promoted Tejano interests by advancing the economic development of Texas, they also abetted Anglo-American colonization efforts.[3]

Navarro's support of legislation favorable to Texas reached a crossroad when the San Antonio Tejano electorate chose him and his uncle José Francisco Ruiz as delegates to the 1836 Convention for Texas Independence. Even though he had previously promoted the interests of Texas within the Mexican political system, the independence of Texas declared at that Convention marked a definitive split from Mexican rule. No doubt Navarro recognized the enormity of this decision. His contemporaries later testified that "he trembled at the thought of having to sanction with his signature the eternal separation of Texas from the mother-country." Nonetheless, Navarro's signature on the Declaration of Independence from Mexico, along with his subsequent leadership role in drafting the Constitution of the Republic of Texas, clearly indicate his alignment with Anglo Americans against the Mexican government.[4]

Five years later, Navarro served as a commissioner in the Santa Fe expedition, an effort organized by Texas president Mirabeau Buonaparte Lamar to incorporate eastern New Mexico into the Republic of Texas. Mexican authorities captured Navarro and the other members of this expedition. Subsequently they convicted Navarro of treason and imprisoned him for four years. Navarro's rationale for accepting the role of commissioner in this ill-fated venture is subject to debate. One of his contemporaries later wrote that he "accepted the appointment [as commissioner] with misgiving, and only at the earnest solicitation of the President," and even suggested that Navarro "felt that in case of success he might prove a useful protector to a Mexican population brought suddenly under the military control of another race." Some observers claim Navarro prepared a strong pro-Texas speech to deliver in New Mexico, although it appears that he merely translated the document in question. In any event, his participation as commissioner in the Santa Fe expedition illustrates the assistance he offered Anglo-American political leaders in Texas.[5]

Tejano Advocate

After Texas independence, Navarro defended Tejano interests in a political system controlled by Anglo Americans, usually as the sole Tejano representative to elected bodies. Although his biographers rarely recognize Navarro's initiatives on behalf of his Tejano constituency, these initiatives overshadow his support of Anglo-American concerns.

Navarro was not always successful in his efforts on behalf of his fellow Tejanos, particularly in his attempts to protect Tejano land claims. As a San Antonio representative to the national congress of the Republic of Texas in 1839, he pleaded in vain for the enactment of legislation which would have aided Tejanos who had no title to their lands, could not speak English, and lacked the finances and familiarity with the legal system necessary for lawsuits. At the Texas Constitutional Convention before U.S. annexation in 1845, Navarro participated in lengthy debates about land grants enacted under the governments of Spain, Mexico, and the Republic of Texas. He argued that his opponents' excessive requirements to validate previous land titles denied long-standing land owners their legitimate claims. Exasperated with the overwhelming opposition mounted against him, Navarro offered a final satirical protest against their position; he suggested that the Constitution of the State of Texas require these owners to confirm their land grants by enclosing them with stone fences at least eight yards in height! Later as state senator of Texas (1846-1848) and as a private citizen, Navarro continued to plead "the cause of the old settlers of Texas, who are wantonly attacked by those who come into the country with their clean hands, to snatch from them the fruits [of land ownership] acquired by perseverance and fortitude." Despite Navarro's tireless efforts, many Tejanos lost their ancestral lands after U.S. annexation.[6]

In other instances, Navarro's legislative efforts were successful. At the 1845 Texas Constitutional Convention, there was heated debate about the proposal that suffrage be extended exclusively to the "free white population." A speech made by Francis Moore, Jr. of Harris County left no doubt that for some delegates this was meant to disfranchise Tejanos:

> Strike out the term "white," and what will be the result? Hordes of Mexican Indians may come in here from the West, and may be more formidable than the enemy you have vanquished. Silently they will come moving in; they will come back in thousands to Béxar, in thousands to Goliad, perhaps to Nacogdoches, and what will be the consequence? Ten, twenty, thirty, forty, fifty thousand may come in here, and vanquish you at the ballot box.

Navarro contended that including the word "white" in electoral legislation was "odious" and "ridiculous." In the end, the position of Navarro and others held sway, as Tejanos were not denied voting rights in the Constitution of the State of Texas. Perhaps in response to the suffering which the Texas army inflicted on Tejanos during the period of the Texas Republic, Navarro also successfully promoted the following statute in the state constitution: "No soldier shall, in time of peace, be quartered in the house, or within the enclosure of any individual, without the consent of the owner; nor in time of war, but in a manner prescribed by law."[7]

Navarro also defended Tejano citizenship rights against the anti-immigrant, anti-Catholic Know Nothing Party. In San Antonio's municipal elections of 1854, the Know Nothings gained control of the mayoral office and city council. Responding to the Know Nothing victory, the Democratic Party of Béxar County mounted a vigorous organizing campaign during the 1855 state canvass. Spanish-speaking San Antonians held a series of "Democratic Meetings of Mexican-Texan Citizens of Béxar County." At one of these meetings, an open letter from Navarro was read to thunderous applause. Subsequently the letter was published in both the Spanish and English press. Navarro reminded Tejanos that their Hispanic-Mexican ancestors founded their city and built the church in which they worshipped God. Citing Know Nothing anti-Catholic attitudes, he also reminded his audience that "the Mexico-Texans are Catholics, and should be proud of the faith of their ancestors, and defend it inch by inch against such infamous aggressors." He urged them not to let others abuse their "Hispanic-Mexican generosity" and loyalty, nor to make them "traitors" to their political party and the Catholic faith they inherited from their ancestors. Backed by a solid Tejano bloc vote, Democrats won the 1855 elections, besting their Know Nothing opponents by almost three to one among Béxar County voters, thus initiating the decline of Know Nothing Party influence in Texas.[8]

Defending the Tejano Legacy

Despite the efforts of Navarro and other Tejano leaders to defend their people's interests, Tejanos' economic and political influence diminished significantly in San Antonio after U.S. annexation in 1845. They increasingly became a working underclass after statehood and, as previously mentioned, lost most of their land holdings. In the political realm, Tejano electees to the San Antonio city council decreased threefold in the first fifteen years after U.S. annexation. Five of the eight members of the city council were Tejanos in 1845, but in 1860 not a single Tejano served in that capacity.[9]

The economic and political diminishment of Tejanos at San Antonio, along with the corresponding Anglo-American ascendancy, was accompanied by literary attempts to interpret these changes. Anglo Americans tended to interpret their presence in San Antonio as initiating an era of progress. In an 1851 book, for example, Francis Baylies applauded the Franciscans who worked in the San Antonio missions during the eighteenth century, although he incorrectly identified them as Jesuits. Baylies then added:

> After the expulsion of the Jesuits, everything went to decay. Agriculture, learning, the mechanic arts, shared the common fate; and when the banners of the United States were unfurled in these distant and desolate places, the descendants of the noble and chivalric Castilians had sunk to the level, perhaps beneath it, of the aboriginal savages; but it is to be hoped that the advent of the Saxo-Norman may brighten, in some degree, the faded splendor of the race which has fallen.[10]

Similar views of Tejano demise followed by Anglo-American progress appeared in the San Antonio press. Even Anglo Americans who "defended" the Tejano population against public criticism ascribed to the view that Tejanos were victims of a morally and intellectually impoverished heritage, and that Anglo-American influence offered a means to redeem that heritage. Concerned that a *San Antonio Ledger* article attacking the character of local Tejanos might discourage further Anglo-American and European immigration to the city, for example, a correspondent responded in another local newspaper:

> It is lamentably true that our Mexican population, generally, do not occupy as high a position in the scale of morality and intelligence as is desirable; yet every one who knows their former condition, and will take into consideration their former mode of life, as well as the demoralizing effect of the Government under which they lived previous to the establishment of the Texas Republic, must admit that they are reforming as rapidly as could have been expected, under the circumstances by which they have been surrounded.[11]

Navarro led the Tejano response to Anglo-American renderings of their history. Although previously he had recorded only privately some brief remarks on local events during the Mexican War of Independence from Spain, he presented his later writings in the English-language press to correct publicly the Anglo-American historical accounts and biased attitudes. In 1853 he contested a *San Antonio Ledger* account which claimed that "for one hundred years after the expedition of Alonzo de León, the history of San Antonio, as well as of all Texas, is but the dreary register of petty territorial squabbles, barbarous feuds and feats of monkish strategy." According to this article, it was not until the arrival of Anglo Americans that San Antonio "was baptized in the blood of heroism

personified, and consecrated Liberty and imperishable renown."[12]

Navarro's initial response, written in Spanish and translated for the local press, was published in the *Western Texan*
on December 1, 1853. It began by stating: "In the [*Ledger*] issue
of September 17 [15] last, I read some historical recollections
concerning the foundation and early history of San Antonio
de Béxar. Since I was an eyewitness of all the salient events
that were described, I cannot resist the temptation to correct
some substantial errors contained in that narrative." His
account went on to describe Mexico's struggle for independence from Spain, particularly the courage of local Tejanos
during battles between revolutionaries and royalist forces in
1813. Navarro recognized the "glory and valor" of the defenders who later died in the 1836 Alamo battle. But his primary
contention was that San Antonio had an honorable citizenry
with aspirations for a free system of government decades
before that famous battle and that these "noble citizens of
Béxar sacrificed their lives and property, performing heroic
deeds of valor" in the cause of Mexican independence.[13]

Four years later, Navarro published another narrative in
three installments of the *Ledger* in which he described the 1811
efforts for independence by the citizens of San Antonio de
Béxar. This narrative was a response to Henderson Yoakum's
History of Texas (1855), which Navarro claimed was "plagued
by a number of inexactitudes." Another purpose of Navarro's
account was "to inform our Americans, however indignant
some of them among us may be, who with base and aggressive
pretexts want to uproot from this classic land its legitimate
people who are descendants of those whom we now honor."
Outraged by the violence many Tejanos suffered, Navarro
stated at the conclusion of these three installments:

To complete the picture of misfortune [for the San Antonio martyrs for Mexican independence], the few descendants who survive in San Antonio are disappearing, murdered in full view of a people who boast of their justice and excellence . . . . May Divine Providence use these historical commentaries to stir generous hearts to treat with more respect this race of men who, as the legitimate proprietors of this land, lost it together with their lives and their hopes, to follow in the footsteps of those very ones who now enjoy the land in the midst of peace and plenty.[14]

In 1869, Narciso Leal and other friends of Navarro published a Spanish version of his writings in a single volume entitled *Apuntes históricos interesantes de San Antonio de Béxar* (Commentaries of Historical Interest on San Antonio de Béxar). This volume included their biographical sketch of Navarro, along with a letter from Navarro dated June 5, 1869. Navarro's letter states: "My only purpose in writing and publishing [the commentaries] was to eliminate some errors that I had seen published in the American press concerning several episodes occurring in Texas back in the years 1811 and 1813 . . . when for the first time the scions of San Antonio de Béxar manifested their patriotism and performed prodigies of bravery that were almost unbelievable."[15]

Navarro's defense of the Tejano historical legacy reflects his defense of the Tejano right to land claims, the vote, and full citizenship. Written after his retirement from the state senate, Navarro's historical writings continued his earlier advocacy on behalf of his Tejano constituency. As a native San Antonian, his recollections of his people's contribution to San Antonio's historical development undoubtedly strengthened his resolve to resist Anglo-American efforts which denied Tejanos their ancestral lands, their long-standing elective franchise, and their status as full citizens.

Historical works which depict Navarro as an "Americanized Texian" or "Anglocized Mexican" overlook his role as a champion of Tejano rights. Although at times Navarro's political agenda converged with that of Anglo Americans, his vigorous defense of Tejano interests overshadows his support of Anglo-American concerns. The limited biographical works on Navarro to date have not done him justice. While a comprehensive analysis of his life is beyond the scope of this study, clearly any critical biography of Navarro must examine his complex role as a Tejano advocate and historical chronicler.

Navarro's *Apuntes* illustrates that the writing of history has political implications. When Anglo-American writers proffered their versions of Texas history, they contrasted Tejano decline with Anglo-American progress, often as a justification for U.S. expansion. Navarro reminded these newcomers that they built on earlier Tejano achievements, frequently at the expense of native-born Texan residents. His historical commentaries, the first Tejano publication on Texas history, identify the Tejano community as the descendants of a people who developed San Antonio, sacrificed their lives for it, and therefore retained legitimate claims for respect within it, despite the Anglo-American takeover.

Endnotes

[1]J[acob] De Cordova, *Texas: Her Resources and Her Public Men. A Companion for J. De Cordova's New and Correct Map of the State of Texas* (Philadelphia: J. B. Lippincott, 1858), 147; *Biography of José Antonio Navarro, Written by an Old Texan*, with a preface by Mary Bell Hart (Houston: Telegraph Steam, 1876; reprint, [San Antonio]: Hart Graphics, 1976), 10; Frederick Charles Chabot, *With the Makers of San Antonio. Genealogies of the Early Latin, Anglo-American, and German Families with Occasional Biographies, Each Group Being Prefaced with a Brief Historical Sketch and Illustrations* (San Antonio: Artes Graficas, 1937), 203; Naomi Fritz, "José Antonio Navarro" (M.A. thesis, St. Mary's University, San Antonio, 1941), 18; *Handbook of Texas* (Austin: Texas State Historical Association, 1952), 2:262; Joseph Martin Dawson, *José Antonio Navarro: Co-Creator of Texas* (Waco: Baylor University Press, 1969), 1, 31, 34, 61; Thomas Lloyd Miller, "José Antonio Navarro, 1795-1871," *Journal of Mexican American History* 2 (Spring 1972), 77. In a 1978 thesis, Anastacio Bueno, Jr. provides a more balanced treatment of Navarro's public career from 1821-1846. Anastacio Bueno, Jr., "In Storms of Fortune: José Antonio Navarro of Texas, 1821-1846" (M.A. thesis, University of Texas, San Antonio, 1978).

[2]N[arciso] Leal and various friends, "Breve rasgo biográfico sobre el autor de estos apuntes," in José Antonio Navarro, *Apuntes históricos interesantes de San Antonio de Béxar escritos por el C. Dn. José Antonio Navarro, en noviembre de 1853. Y publicados por varios de sus amigos* (San Antonio: Privately printed, 1869), 4. Quotation cited is the authors' translation of the text. Narciso Leal was a San Antonian of Canary Island descent. He was a prominent stockman and merchant, a leader in civic affairs, and a supporter of several short-lived attempts to publish a Spanish-language newspaper at San Antonio. A Confederate lieutenant in the Civil War, Leal subsequently lived more than forty years in his home at 409 S. Flores St., where he died in 1909 at the age of seventy-six. *Bejareño* (San Antonio), 7, 21 July 1855; *San Antonio Ledger*, 14 July 1855; *Correo* (San Antonio), 26 May, 8 July 1858; *San Antonio Express*, 3 December 1868, 3; 6 July 1876, 1, 4; 24 July 1886, 2; 22 February 1909, 5; *Mooney and Morrison's General Directory of the City of San*

Antonio, for 1877-1878 (Galveston: Galveston News Book and Job Office, 1877), 134.

[3]Eugene C. Barker, ed., "Minutes of the *Ayuntamiento* of San Felipe de Austin, 1828-1832," *Southwestern Historical Quarterly* 21 (January 1918): 311; Ramón Músquiz to Stephen F. Austin, 17 April, 15 May 1828, in Eugene C. Barker, ed., *The Austin Papers* (Washington, D.C.: U.S. Government Printing Office, 1924-1928), 2:31, 38; José Antonio Navarro to Austin, 17 May 1828, ibid., 2:41; Miguel Arciniega to Austin, 17 May 1828, ibid., 2:41-42; Andrés Tijerina, *Tejanos and Texas under the Mexican Flag, 1821-1836* (College Station: Texas A&M University Press, 1994), 115-16. Quotation cited from Navarro correspondence is the authors' translation of the text. Further correspondence between Navarro and Austin which illuminates their mutually beneficial relationship is in Barker, ed., *The Austin Papers*, vols. 1-2. The law Navarro presented was passed by the state legislature on May 5, 1828. H. P. N. Gammel, comp., *The Laws of Texas, 1822-1897* (Austin: Gammel Book Co., 1898), 1:103. For a fuller account of Navarro's activities during the period of the Mexican Republic, see Bueno, "In Storms of Fortune," 30-79.

[4]De Cordova, *Texas*, 150 (quotation); R[euben] M. Potter, *The Texas Revolution: Distinguished Mexicans Who Took Part in the Revolution of Texas, with Glances at Its Early Events*, 9; Statement of William Menefee, in Sam Houston Dixon, *The Men Who Made Texas Free* (Houston: Texas Historical Publishing, 1924), 243-44. Potter's work is reprinted from the *Magazine of American History* (October 1878) and is available at The Center for American History, University of Texas at Austin (CAH). Menefee made his comments on Navarro in an 1875 interview. Dixon, *The Men Who Made Texas Free*, 227-28.

[5]Potter, *The Texas Revolution*, 21 (quotations); Rena Maverick Green, ed., *Memoirs of Mary A. Maverick* (San Antonio: Alamo, 1921), 58. The claim that Navarro prepared a strong pro-Texas speech is in Anonymous, "To the Inhabitants of Santa Fe and Other Towns of New Mexico East of the Rio Grande" (typescript), Daughters of the Republic of Texas Library, San Antonio; "Señor Navarro Tells the Story of His Grandfather," in *Rise of the Lone Star: A Story of Texas Told by Its Pioneers*, ed. Howard R. Driggs and Sarah S. King (New York: Frederick A. Stokes, 1936), 289. This claim is contradicted by a letter written during the preparations for the Santa

Fe expedition. Reuben M. Potter to M[irabeau] B[uonaparte] Lamar, 5 June 1841, in *The Papers of Mirabeau Buonaparte Lamar*, ed. Charles Adams Gulick, Jr. and Katherine Elliott (Austin: Von Boeckmann-Jones, 1973), 3:532-33.

[6] *Houston Telegraph and Texas Register*, 26 January 1839; William F. Weeks, comp., *Debates of the Texas Convention* (Houston: J. W. Cruger, 1846), 410-11, 714-16, 738; *Journals of the Senate of the First Legislature of the State of Texas* (Clarksville: Standard, 1848), 203-205; Navarro to Messrs. Cruger and Moore, 12 August 1848, in *Houston Telegraph and Texas Register*, 30 November 1848 (quotation). No legislation passed during Navarro's term at the Third Congress of the Republic of Texas reflects his 1839 intervention on behalf of Tejano land owners. Gammel, comp., *Laws of Texas*, 2:3-167. Although incomplete, the 1840 census showed that Tejanos owned 85.1 percent of the town lots at San Antonio, along with 63.8 percent of land claims with completed titles. On the 1850 census, however, they owned only 9.1 percent of real estate values claimed, and only 7.8 percent on the 1860 census. Gifford White, ed., *The 1840 Census of the Republic of Texas*, with a foreword by James M. Day (Austin: Pemberton, 1966), 12-18; V. K. Carpenter, comp., *The State of Texas Federal Population Schedules Seventh Census of the United States, 1850* (Huntsville, Arkansas: Century Enterprises, 1969), 1:111-89; "Population Schedules of the Eighth Census of the United States, 1860" (Washington: The National Archives, 1967, text-fiche), roll 1288:1-192a.

[7] Weeks, comp., *Debates of the Texas Convention*, 235, 158, 473-74. Tejano suffering from the violence of Texas volunteers during the period of the Texas Republic is treated in Timothy M. Matovina, *Tejano Religion and Ethnicity: San Antonio, 1821-1860* (Austin: University of Texas Press, 1995), 30-33.

[8] *Texas State Times* (Austin), 6 January 1855; *San Antonio Texan* 21, 28 June, 12 July 1855; *Texas State Gazette* (Austin), 25 July 1855; *Bejareño* (San Antonio), 23 June, 7, 21 (quotations) July 1855; *San Antonio Ledger*, 14, 21 July 1855; Sister Paul of the Cross McGrath, "Political Nativism in Texas, 1825-1860" (Ph.D. diss., Catholic University of America, Washington, D.C., 1930), 98-102. Quotations cited are the authors' translation of text. The translation in the *Ledger* has several inaccuracies. For a treatment of Know Nothing activity in San Antonio, see Matovina, *Tejano Religion and Ethnicity*, 70-74.

[9]The 1830 census showed that most of San Antonio's overwhelmingly Tejano population were farmers and only 14.8 percent were laborers. No employment figures are available from the 1840 census, which lists land holders only and does not indicate the overall population. According to the 1850 census, local Tejanos comprised less than half of the city's population for the first time since the foundation of San Antonio de Béxar, and 61.4 percent of the Tejanos were in labor positions. Tabulations from 1860 indicate that this latter number had risen slightly to 65 percent and that Tejanos were a little less than one third of San Antonio's 7,643 free residents. Gifford White, *1830 Citizens of Texas* (Austin: Eakin, 1983), 79-112; Carpenter, comp., *The State of Texas Federal Population Schedules Seventh Census of the United States, 1850,* 1:111-89; "Population Schedules of the Eighth Census of the United States, 1860," roll 1288:1-192a. In the 1850 and 1860 census, the majority of Tejano laborers were cartmen. Contemporary travelers to San Antonio also noted the predominance of Tejano cartmen. See, *e.g.,* Frederick Law Olmsted, *A Journey Through Texas; or, A Saddle-Trip on the Southwestern Frontier: With a Statistical Appendix* (New York: Dix, Edwards & Co., 1857), 152-53, 160; John Russell Bartlett, *Personal Narrative of Explorations and Incidents in Texas, New Mexico, California, Sonora, and Chihuahua, Connected with the United States and Mexican Boundary Commission, During the Years 1850, '51, '52, and '53* (New York: D. Appleton, 1854; reprint, Chicago: Rio Grande Press, 1965), 1:40. Tejano electees to the San Antonio city council accounted for 73.2 percent of the total during the period of the Texas Republic (1836-1845) but only 24.2 percent during the first fifteen years after U.S. annexation. "Minutes of the City Council of the City of San Antonio from 1837 to 1849, Journal A" (typescript), CAH; "Journal of City Council B: January 1849 to August 1856, City of San Antonio," City Clerk's Office, San Antonio; "Journal of City Council C, April 1, 1856 to Feb. 21, 1870, City of San Antonio," ibid. Census data demonstrating Tejanos' loss of their land holdings was given above in note 6.

[10]Francis Baylies, *A Narrative of Major General Wool's Campaign in Mexico, in the Years 1846, 1847 & 1848* (Albany: Little, 1851; reprint, Austin: Jenkins, 1975), 11. Earlier works on Texas history by Anglo Americans had already articulated this thesis. See, *e.g.,* C[hester] Newell, *History of the Revolution in Texas, Particularly of the War of 1835 & '36; Together with the Latest Geographical, Topographical, and Statistical Accounts of the Country, from the Most*

Authentic Sources (New York: Wiley & Putnam, 1838), 13-14; L. T. Pease, "A Geographical and Historical View of Texas; with a Detailed Account of the Texian Revolution and War," in John M. Niles, *History of South America and Mexico; Comprising Their Discovery, Geography, Politics, Commerce, and Revolutions* (Hartford: H. Huntington, 1838), 1:252-54; William Kennedy, *Texas: The Rise, Progress, and Prospects of the Republic of Texas* (London: R. Hastings, 1841; reprint, Fort Worth: Molyneaux Craftsmen, 1925), 233-34; Arthur Ikin, *Texas: Its History, Topography, Agriculture, Commerce, and General Statistics. To Which Is Added, a Copy of the Treaty of Commerce Entered into by the Republic of Texas and Great Britain. Designed for the Use of the British Merchant, and as a Guide to Emigrants* (London: Sherwood, Gilbert, and Piper, 1841), 1.

[11] *Western Texan* (San Antonio), 14 October 1852. See also *San Antonio Ledger*, 15 September 1853; *San Antonio Daily Herald*, 15 July 1858. Contemporary scholars have critiqued the tendency of religious and secular historians to present this one-sided perspective of Mexican decline followed by Anglo-American redemption. See, *e.g.*, Gilberto M. Hinojosa, "The Enduring Hispanic Faith Communities: Spanish and Texas Church Historiography," *Journal of Texas Catholic History and Culture* 1 (March 1990), 20-41; Robert E. Wright, "Local Church Emergence and Mission Decline: The Historiography of the Catholic Church in the Southwest During the Spanish and Mexican Periods," *U. S. Catholic Historian* 9 (Winter/Spring 1990), 27-48.

[12] *San Antonio Ledger*, 15 September 1853. The *Ledger* account draws heavily on material from Kennedy, *Texas*, 266-77. For Navarro's earlier writings, see José Antonio Navarro, "José Antonio Navarro, Béxar, [Texas]," 18 May 1841, in Gulick and Elliott, eds., *Papers of Lamar*, 3:525-27; Navarro, "José Antonio Navarro San Antonio de Béxar? [Texas], Autobiographical Notes, [1841?]," ibid., 3:597-98. Apparently Navarro wrote the 1841 documents at the request of President Mirabeau Buonaparte Lamar. Lamar gathered information for a history of Texas which he never completed.

[13] Navarro, *Apuntes*, 13, 14, 19; *Western Texan* (San Antonio), 1 December 1853; "Anonymous. Early History of San Antonio," 1 December 1853, in Gulick and Elliott, eds., *Papers of Lamar*, 4:5, 7, 12. The latter two references do not identify the author of this

account, but it is clearly an English translation of the historical
narrative later attributed to Navarro in *Apuntes*. Quotations cited
are authors' translation from the Spanish edition of *Apuntes*.

[14]Navarro, *Apuntes*, 5, 6, 12; *San Antonio Ledger*, 12 December
1857, 2 January 1858. The other section of this account was in the
Ledger, 19 December 1857. Quotations cited are the authors'
translation from the Spanish edition of *Apuntes*. Navarro wrote his
1857 installments as the Cart War raged. Tejano cartmen were
attacked by their competitors in retaliation for underbidding them.
Navarro protested the murder of one such victim, Antonio
Delgado, in his January 2 installment. For a treatment of the Cart
War, see Dorothy Kelly Gibson, "Social Life in San Antonio,
1855-1860" (M.A. thesis, University of Texas, Austin, 1937), 14-17;
J. Fred Rippy, "Border Troubles Along the Rio Grande, 1848-1860,"
Southwestern Historical Quarterly 23 (October 1919): 103-104; John
J. Linn, *Reminiscences of Fifty Years in Texas* (New York: D. & J.
Sadlier, 1883; reprint, Austin: State House Press, 1986), 352-54.
Yoakum's 1855 work cited Navarro's 1853 account as a source.
H[enderson] Yoakum, *History of Texas, from Its First Settlement in
1685 to Its Annexation to the United States in 1846* (New York:
Redfield, 1855; reprint, Austin: Steck, 1935), 1:168-70, 176.

[15]Navarro to Narciso Leal and his friends, 5 June 1869, in
Navarro, *Apuntes*, 2.

The Commentaries

Introductory Letters

Narciso Leal and his friends secured Navarro's permission to publish a Spanish version of Apuntes *in 1869. They also wrote a biographical sketch of Navarro. This supportive material is presented here in English translation.*

San Antonio, June 5, 1869

To citizen and Colonel[1] José Antonio Navarro:
Dear Sir and Friend of Ours:

When the interesting historical commentaries, written by you years ago, finally arrived in our hands, we did not hesitate one instant in publishing them in the press for the widest distribution. Consequently, we ask of you this time[2] to set aside your scrupulous modesty and favor our idea of publishing your historical commentaries, for we believe firmly they will be received with enthusiasm by all Mexican citizens of Texas, especially the descendants of San Antonio.

We do not doubt the insufficiency of the analogous commentary that we must add to this important document. Nevertheless, again, we beg you to assent to our taking this liberty and consider that our desire to publish your commentaries, which obliges us to produce those essays, is greater than our confidence in our knowledge.

Your obedient servants Q.B.S.M.[3]

N[arciso] Leal[4] and several friends

Mr. Narciso Leal and friends,
San Antonio, June 5, 1869

Dear Gentlemen of my consideration,

I have received your kind letter and am apprised of its content. I would reply saying that, beginning in the years of 1853, or 1857, I believe, I wrote two small works which, because there was no Castilian press in this city, I sought to have published in English translation, which is how they came to light.

My only purpose in writing and publishing them was to eliminate some errors that I had seen published in the American press concerning several episodes occurring in Texas back in the years 1811 and 1813. These years were most fertile in politics and impassioned events concerning Mexican independence, when for the first time the scions of San Antonio de Béxar manifested their patriotism and performed prodigies of bravery that were almost unbelievable. The descendants of those noble [Canary] Islanders, such as the Delgados, Traviesos, Arochas, Leales, and other patriots of the same stature took an active part in these events.

I have always thought that it would be very beneficial for posterity to know from a contemporary eyewitness about the achievements, sacrifices, and the tragic end that their illustrious ancestors suffered in that struggle to win Mexican independence and liberty. It was for this reason that I published these two works and left them to the public domain. Consequently you are at absolute liberty to do with them what you please.

Nevertheless, I remain very appreciative of the courtesy that you have gratuitously shown to obtain the acquiescence of this your very attentive servant.

José Antonio Navarro

A Brief Biographical Sketch
Of The Author Of These Commentaries

There are few men like José Antonio Navarro, who have not only desired to be a patriot but have known how to be one—which is what makes a citizen illustrious. We will not attempt to make Mr. Navarro appear as a liberator, like Bolivar; nor a jurisprudent like Henry Clay; nor a leader like Hidalgo, because the knowledge we have of his irrepressible dignity forbids it. But we can assure that his return to private life has made him a greater man than fame would have made of him in the spacious halls of the senate.

Despite his scant education, José Antonio Navarro is one of those men who stands out, even alongside other men of note. We can say that his intellect has little in common with the others, but comes very close to that of B[enjamin] Franklin. Everyone knows more of the virtues than of the talent of the Philadelphia philosopher. José Antonio appears to be of this mold, having made himself worthy of the merit conceded to him by all those who have the opportunity to deal with him in good faith. Whoever treats with Mr. Navarro diligently, in accord with his ideas, or who upon meeting him engages his sense of humor, is received by José Antonio and treated with a tact and courtesy that leaves nothing to be desired.

The furniture and various items which make up the contents of his home immediately convey the idea that this honorable compatriot is a member of that small body of men whose simple and unchanging customs embody both knowledge and recreation. This is an enrapturing thing that imposes equally the austerity of science with spirited associations and friendship, as though they existed in perfect harmony.

To see José Antonio, at the age at which we write these paragraphs, is to recall the saying: "so young yet so old." His appearance is of the Spanish type. He has an aquiline nose, a pure ruddy color of face, and the uniform whiteness of his complete head of hair delicately frames his wide forehead. But nothing of his physiognomy shows the excesses of premature age. To the contrary, his sane judgment and his intelligence—clear and quick to perceive—his natural voice, energetic and sonorous when he raises it, with its facile action and accent, enables the least observant person to see that José Antonio Navarro is in the prime of his golden years. Consequently he possesses a high level of energy to live his life with perfected harmony—amazing results of a frugal life balanced by wholesome customs.

Many times those of us writing these lines have had the good fortune of spending a few hours at the side of this honorable elder without considering it to be more than a very useful and agreeable company that influences our soul in the regions of pleasure and the unknown. Alexander of Russia said one night, in the Theater of Erfurth to Napoleon himself:

"The friendship of a great man
    is a favor of the Gods."

And how many times would we have missed a new idea, if we had not been listening to the reason of the sound intelligence of our venerable friend!

Of course we would over extend ourselves if we tried to consider all the points to make a more complete [biography]—which could easily fill this brief note. But we are satisfied that there are persons who probably should be working on a complete biography of José Antonio, and we leave that task to them as being more competent and better informed than we are. However, we can only conclude with a

José Antonio Navarro, ca. 1860s.
Courtesy Casa Navarro State Historical Park, San Antonio.

limited account of the birth and some of the events of the life of our subject.

José Antonio Navarro was born in this city on February 27, 1795. His parents were Angel Navarro,[5] a native of Corsica (Europe), and María Josefa Ruiz y Peña,[6] of Spanish origin and a creole of this city. As a person whom nature had chosen for great and righteous ideas, José Antonio quickly absorbed the scant education that he was able to obtain in the state of Coahuila.[7] But because of his desire to learn, he knew that was not enough and he persevered. Trust in the faith of self-education was how Don José Antonio has been called to occupy distinguished positions first in Mexico, then in the Republic of Texas, and later in the United States.

The life of José Antonio Navarro can be divided into three glorious epochs: (1) that of his birth and youth in Mexican Texas, where at a very young age he was initiated in the events of the insurrection according to the *commentaries* that follow. (2) That of his mature age, in which he figured notably in the revolution of Republican Texas, in which because of the firmness of his character and principles, he experienced a cruel *deception* by Santa Anna, the most despotic of the dictators of Mexico. (3) Consequently, for the remainder of his days, from then until the present time, he has continued to be the strongest champion of the rights of the people in the United States—not withstanding his retirement from public events that today agitate the country. This is how our venerable compatriot lives today, providing with his disciplined conduct and orderly habits the most relevant example of good sense in the question of political parties.

José Antonio Navarro has many prestigious friends in this country who take pleasure in recalling his merit, not withstanding any opposition to his political beliefs.

There are instances of men more eminent than he, who

by reason of their knowledge and youth bask in the fame of illustrious audiences who then disappear like the lightning that only lasts for the rainy season. But José Antonio, following the course of events, has imparted to his country the enduring service of his virtuous life and common sense that is only given to the predestined.

Such is our perspective of the life of the H[onorable] and worthy elder. At seventy-four years of age, it appears that the increase of time weighs upon him only to enhance the marvelous memory he possesses. The lesion on the left leg, caused by an accident in the year [year omitted],[8] resulted in a painful tumor that aggravates his suffering. Nevertheless, this condition has not prevented our venerable fellow citizen from the exercise of walking naturally and regularly.

We will conclude this article, whose purpose is to highlight the character of the author of the *Historical Commentaries,* which we have the pleasure to present to our fellow citizens as an endowment of our country's past. Yet at the same time other facts about José Antonio Navarro must be withheld because of his scrupulous modesty that would not pardon us, in spite of the consent he gives in his answer to our letter at the beginning of this booklet.

Let the foregoing be sufficient for all who know the H[onorable] José Antonio Navarro to understand that we have written in deference to the truth, which medium we hope will serve as a declaration for all those who, like us, profess a true affection for him.

San Antonio June 20, 1869.

N[arciso] Leal and several friends

Western Texan, (San Antonio), 1 December 1853.

Navarro wrote his first published historical commentary in response to a San Antonio Ledger *article of September 1853. This response, intended for Anglo-American readers, was translated into English. The original Spanish version was published in 1869. Numerous errors and mistranslations are evident in the extant translations. To ensure the greatest accuracy, the 1869 Spanish edition has been translated here.*

Historical Commentaries of San Antonio de Bexar by an Eyewitness.

To the Editor of the *San Antonio Ledger*:

Respectable Sir:

In the issue of September 15 last,[9] I read some historical recollections concerning the foundation and early history of San Antonio de Béxar. Since I was an eyewitness of all the salient events that were described, I cannot resist the temptation to correct some substantial errors contained in that narrative. Undoubtedly, they are the result of inaccurate reports which were perhaps taken from mutilated and incomplete documents from which it was difficult to follow the historical chronology.[10] An accurate chronicle of those events has long been needed, for it would present to posterity the customs, character, abilities and moral qualities of the men of that epoch.

In 1813, the author of this letter was nearly eighteen years old; he lived in San Antonio and still retains fresh memories of that time. This circumstance, and his passion for his beloved

San Antonio's history (which should be narrated with due respect for the truth) has produced the present declaration.

You will not discover vainglory, nor the inordinate desire for excellence of style, but rather a concise narrative of bloody and revolutionary times. The Mexican priest named Miguel Hidalgo y Costilla, embellished by a thousand superlatives, was the first to utter the cry of independence in the town of Dolores. The priest José María Morelos, famous from that time to the present for his military talents, was another one of the heroes of Mexican independence. After the execution of the priest Hidalgo, Morelos convened the first Mexican Congress at Apatzingán.[11] General Félix María Calleja, later Viceroy of Mexico, was particularly notorious for his bloody persecutions and iniquities against the patriots Hidalgo, Guerrero, Morelos, Bravo and others. Calleja was the most formidable enemy the Mexicans had.

Morelos was captured, humiliated, and finally shot in the old castle of San Cristóbal, four leagues distance from the capital of Mexico.

José Bernardo Gutiérrez, a native of Revilla,[12] Tamaulipas, fled to the United States immediately after the capture and imprisonment of the patriot heroes in Acatita de Baján near Monclova in the year 1811.

He went to Washington and other cities in the United States, and finally in the state of Louisiana he assembled four hundred fifty American volunteers with whom he again invaded Texas, in the month of October 1812.

Nacogdoches, a military fortification on the Trinity River,[13] was captured by him without resistance, and subsequently he took La Bahía del Espíritu Santo, known today as Goliad. In response, Manuel Salcedo,[14] military governor of Texas, and Simón de Herrera of Nuevo León,[15] rode out with more than two thousand men and attacked La Bahía on

November 15 of the same year.

Generals Gutiérrez, Mc.Gee [Magee], Kemper, Perry, and Ross[16] sustained the siege for three vexatious months; almost all their force was composed of American volunteers and some Mexicans. Finally, in desperation they came out from the walls of Goliad and fought the enemy. They returned to the fort having suffered almost no losses, leaving two hundred of the enemy dead and wounded. Toward the end of March 1813, after twenty-seven regular skirmishes, Salcedo and Herrera discontinued the siege and turned back toward San Antonio. Gutiérrez, Kemper, and the others, encouraged by the forced retreat of the enemy, followed them day by day. Salcedo had barely arrived at San Antonio with his army when Simón de Herrera ordered him to leave the city and march to Salado Creek where, at the place called "Rosillo,"[17] he fought the army of Gutiérrez—if a band of nine hundred patriots could be called such.

The two forces met at the end of March. It was a bloody battle. Herrera lost four hundred men, dead and wounded; Gutiérrez only five dead and fourteen wounded. The royal army ran in disarray toward San Antonio, which Salcedo and Herrera had begun to fortify for the purpose of resisting Gutiérrez.

This Kemper and others, after collecting the spoils of battle and burying the dead, pursued them with their victorious army and took possession of Concepción Mission, southeast of San Antonio. The next day they marched to San Antonio. The army of patriots formed in double columns in the lower *labor*[18] where at present stand the private residences of Devine, Callaghan, and Gilbeau. From that memorable precinct, Bernardo Gutiérrez demanded the unconditional surrender of Governors Salcedo and Herrera. This took place on March 30, 1813. On the afternoon of the 31st, these same

persons with their entire military staff and other officers of
high rank left Béxar on foot and met Gutiérrez and his
victorious army. The conference between victor and van-
quished was brief. Nothing is known about what was said,
except for the request that their lives be guaranteed. Gutiérrez
replied evasively but indicated that their lives were not in
danger.

This cowardly surrender sealed the doom of those unfortunate Spanish officers. They surrendered their swords and
were placed between two columns. Gutiérrez and his army
crossed to the eastern side of the river, compelling their
prisoners to march in front to the sound of martial music, and
they entered within the walls of the Alamo—the same Alamo
which in March 1836 was to become the cradle of the liberty
of Texas and the scene of glory and valor. There, the valiant
patriots Gutiérrez, Kemper, Ross, and their brave companions enjoyed the first sleep since the triumph of March 31st,
and there they sealed the mysterious legacy of those terrible
events which happened in the year of 1836.

On April 1st, at nine in the morning, the republican army
marched to a beating drum from the Alamo to the main plaza
of San Antonio. They crossed the river by means of a miserable bridge, replaced today by the excellent and beautiful one
at Commerce Street. The Hispanic-Mexican army had dis-
banded and retreated the previous night and could not be
found in any part of the city. Only a few persons immobilized
by terror and the families of a some citizens of San Antonio
remained.

Gutiérrez took possession of the Casas Reales,[19] where
the beautiful store of the Vances now stands. He immediately
called an administrative junta or civil council of those citizens
who, with the greater ardor, had opposed Spanish rule and
who consequently had favored Mexican independence. The

The Casas Reales, seat of Spanish government in Texas, faced San Fernando Church from the east side of Main Plaza. It was the scene of dramatic seizures of power, described by Navarro, that occurred during the revolution of 1811-1813. Courtesy of Bexar County and the Witte Museum, San Antonio.

junta was composed of a president, a secretary, and eight to ten members. From the writing of Gutiérrez it seems that he created it with the sole object of court-martialing and sentencing the Spanish prisoners.

The secretary of this junta, Mariano Rodríguez,[20] is still living. At that time he was an active and jolly youth. Today he is an antiquated septuagenarian who merely exists in San Antonio with a very limited recollection of the past and an utter indifference for the future. On the fourth day of April, or possibly on the night of the fifth, a group of sixty Mexican men under the command of Antonio Delgado led fourteen Spanish prisoners, including four of Mexican birth, out of San

Antonio to the eastern bank of Salado Creek, near the same spot where the battle of Rosillo occurred. There they dismounted from their fine horses, with no other arms than the big knives[21] that each of those monsters carried hanging from their belts for use in the country. After having heaped offensive words and insulting epithets upon them, they cut their throats. With inhuman mockery some of those assassins sharpened their knives on the soles of their shoes in the presence of their defenseless victims.

Oh, shame of the human race! Oh disgrace for the descendants of a Christian nation! What people can coolly suffer in silence an act unparalleled in the annals of the history of San Antonio de Béxar? But we owe an impartial history to posterity, that such horrible deeds may be known to the future generations so that through their own good conduct, they may eradicate such horrible stains from our benevolent soil.

One day after the slaughter, I myself saw that horde of assassins arrive with their officer, Antonio Delgado, who halted in front of the Casas Reales to inform Bernardo Gutiérrez that the fourteen victims[22] had been dispatched. On that portentious morning, a large number of other young spectators and I stood at the door of the Casas Reales and watched Captain Delgado's entrance into the hall. He doffed his hat in the presence of General Gutiérrez and, stuttering, he uttered some words mingled with shame. He handed Gutiérrez a paper which, I believe, contained a list of those whose throats had been cut,[23] and whose names I give below:

SPANIARDS:
Manuel Salcedo, Governor
Simón de Herrera, Colonel
Geronimo Herrera, Colonel
Juan Echevarría, Captain[24]

José Mateos, Lieutenant
José Goescochea, Lieutenant
Juan Ignacio Arrambide, Lieutenant
Gregorio Amador, Lieutenant
Antonio López, Lieutenant
Francisco Pereira [Perciva], Captain

MEXICANS:
Miguel de Areos, Captain
Luis Hijo
Juan Caso, Lieutenant[25]

I myself saw the clothing and the blood-stained adorn-
ments which those tigers carried hanging from their saddle
horns, boasting publicly of their crime and of having divided
the spoils among themselves in shares.

As I have said, it is certain that Gutiérrez received in the
same Government House[26] an account of that cruel affair,
although later he disavowed taking part in the execution of
the prisoners. Gutiérrez says in a manuscript which he wrote
and printed in Monterrey on May 26, 1827[27] that he had never
given the order to execute those unfortunate fourteen prisoners, but rather that a great number of citizens, who were
greatly excited and angry with the Spanish governors, induced
a majority of the junta to pass a formal order requiring the
guard who had custody of the prisoners to hand them over
immediately.

The guards, Gutiérrez adds, could do no less than obey
without hesitation—even though an authorization and order
for it should have been prepared. Thus the prisoners under
their responsibility were immediately taken out and conducted to the place where an inhuman and bloody death
awaited them—a death which was given to them without

authorization and without the temporal and spiritual assistance which the Holy Church requires. Perhaps God permitted it as a merited punishment for the inhuman cruelties which had been committed by those unfortunate individuals.

Whoever knows, or who can formulate a rough idea of the type of men of that epoch, can comprehend the extreme depth of ignorance and ferocious passions of the men of those times. Whoever is informed will understand that among the Mexicans of that time, with some exceptions, there was no clear political sentiment. They did not know the importance of the words "independence and liberty" and they did not understand the reasons for the rebellion of the priest Hidalgo as other than a shout for death and a war without quarter on the *gachupines*, as the Spaniards were called. Thus one will readily concede and agree, as Bernardo Gutiérrez has admitted in his own way, that the band of so-called patriots "killed those fourteen victims." But his excuse is very weak, very cowardly, and unworthy of a general who neither would nor could avoid such a scandal, much less relinquish his command upon seeing his cause blackened by a more monstrous action than could be perpetrated by a vandal chieftain. Consequently, Gutiérrez shared in the atrocity. His own dissimulation exposed him, and like Pilate he washed his hands. It was no court martial that sentenced them [Salcedo and the others], as has been erroneously stated.

Kemper and his American auxiliaries were horrified by such a barbarous deed and prepared to leave the country, demanding of Gutiérrez what they were owed in the name of the Mexican Republic. But due to the pleadings of Colonel Miguel Menchaca and other Mexican leaders, they consented to remain in San Antonio to help the cause for Mexican independence.

A few days after these events, it became known with

San Fernando Church. José Antonio Navarro and other youths watched the 1813 Battle of Alazán with field glasses from the church tower. Courtesy *San Antonio Light* collection, The Institute of Texan Cultures, San Antonio.

certainty that Colonel Ignacio Elizondo was marching from [Presidio del] Rio Grande[28] toward San Antonio with an army of more than two thousand men. He was furious about the news of the deaths of the two governors, and by forced marches he arrived at the place known as the Alazán[29] about two miles west of San Antonio.

Gutiérrez and Perry met him there June 3, 1813, and a number of curious youths observed from the towers of the Catholic parish church.[30] We watched the clash of flashing weapons through our field glasses and listened to the horrifying thunder of the cannons.

After four hours of combat Elizondo was defeated and he

abandoned the field of battle, leaving four hundred men dead, wounded and as prisoners. Gutiérrez lost twenty-two men and forty-two wounded. Among the dead was the aide-de-camp Mr. Maricos,[31] a French youth, skillful, learned, courageous, and so gallant that not even the marshals of Napoleon could rival him. The victorious Gutiérrez and Perry had scarcely returned to San Antonio when it was learned that the Commander in Chief of the province, Joaquín de Arredondo, was at Laredo marching toward San Antonio with more than three thousand of the best Mexican troops, including the fugitives of the battles of Alazán who with the defeated Colonel Elizondo had joined them on the road.

At this time, Gutiérrez, despite his victories, began to lose the confidence of his officers and soldiers. Perhaps it was because of his barbarous and abnormal conduct towards the murdered Spaniards, or perhaps because of the political intrigue of José Alvarez de Toledo,[32] a Spaniard who had been sent by the Cortes of Cádiz[33] to the island of San Domingo. Liberal and disaffected with the rule of the king of Spain, he came to Texas from the state of Louisiana to dispossess Gutiérrez of his command. The morale of the republican officers and the army was affected, and what is absolutely certain is that Gutiérrez' influence diminished with the same rapidity it was won in a thousand triumphant battles.

Discouraged on seeing himself abandoned, Gutiérrez left Béxar for the United States with some of his most intimate friends. A few days later, General Toledo took command of the army. Gutiérrez, in his proclamation of May 25, 1827,[34] said that General Alvarez de Toledo was only a sham patriot of Mexican Independence; that when he came to Texas to take command of the republican troops he was in secret correspondence with the king of Spain in an attempt to hinder the progress and the success of the patriots.

It is given as proof that some time after the year 1813, Alvarez de Toledo returned to Spain and was not only received by Fernando VII but was even rewarded with the appointment as ambassador to one of the European courts. Whether this is true or not is a mystery hidden in the obscurity of time long passed. What is at least proved is that, having been a sincere patriot in 1813, Toledo suffered the weakness of taking refuge in the amnesty and favor of the king.[35] But if we may judge by reputation and appearances, we must admit that the assertions about Gutiérrez are supported by the epithets that his own countrymen have hurled in his face: "He was a politician without principles, an uncultured judge, and an insubordinate soldier who was cruel to the marrow."

On the other hand, Toledo was a young man of about thirty-two years, of liberal principles, eloquent in speech and personal gallantry, having resourcefulness, fine manners and diplomacy. With this multitude of seductive qualities he immediately captured the hearts and minds of the army and the residents of San Antonio and later took command as chief as has been said.

At last General Arredondo arrived, furious and impatient to quiet the spirit of insurrection and to avenge the death of his compatriots, the governors. On the 18th of August, and not on the 13th as has been previously reported, Toledo offered to do battle at Medina.[36] This general had fifteen hundred men including six hundred American volunteers; Arredondo had four thousand men. The battle was fought with great military skill on both sides. The American volunteers formed the regiment of infantry and handled the artillery, composed of nine cannons from four to eight caliber.[37] The cavalry consisted of inhabitants of San Antonio and vicinity and of some individuals from Tamaulipas and [Presidio del] Rio Grande.

As a strategic device, Arredondo caused his army to raise a unanimous shout of "Long live the king! Victory is ours!" At the same time the band sounded notes of victory,[38] causing the cavalry of terrorized patriots to flee from the field. However the plodding American infantry and its artillery sustained the deadly fire from Arredondo's eighteen heavy-caliber cannons for more than four hours.

They could not overcome the impossible, nor is it the natural order of things to fight against a disproportionately large force.

Resolving to give themselves up to fate, the American infantry finally abandoned the artillery and hurriedly fled from the field of battle, breaking their rifles against the oak and mesquite trees rather than leave them as trophies for the enemy. Arredondo's cavalry pursued them for six long miles, with saber in hand and fixed lances, inflicting terrible losses. And thus perished the greater part of those brave compatriots.

On the following day, Arredondo entered the city triumphantly, his carts laden with wounded and dying. At this point my hand trembles in recording the scenes of horror which they inflicted even on the bitterest enemies of Gutiérrez in repayment for his past cruelties. Arredondo avenged himself in the most outrageous manner and indiscriminately ordered the imprisonment of seven hundred peaceful inhabitants of San Antonio.

At the same time, he imprisoned three hundred unfortunate people in the cells of the Catholic priests on the night of August 20th. They were crowded like sheep in the fold during the hottest months of summer. On the morning of the following day, eighteen of them had perished from suffocation. The remainder were passed before firing squads, from day to day, for no more reason than having been accused of favoring independence.

By an inexplicable coincidence, it appears that in San Antonio those same places where so many cruelties were committed have been reserved by Providence and destined, in happier times, to serve as lessons in devotion, justice, education, and recreation. For where the courthouse stands today,[39] and in the front of the balustrade of the hotel on the main plaza[40]—one a sanctuary of law, the other a lodging place that provides the most delicious things that gastronomy has to offer—is where in those times daily executions took place, and often the moans of the dying were heard. The post office is the means by which our inner thoughts are communicated in writing, and through which knowledge and civility are diffused through the community; where the post office stands today,[41] Arredondo devised a large prison for women known as *la quinta*.[42]

More than five hundred married and single women whose husbands and fathers were known as insurgents suffered there. For four months, insolent guards daily compelled them to convert twenty-four bushels of corn into tortillas to feed the officers and soldiers of Arredondo. There the modest and sensitive wives and daughters were exposed to the jeers of those depraved, undisciplined troops, and frequently they suffered the impure, lewd gazes and debasing remarks of officers and soldiers who enjoyed that detestable and repugnant spectacle. Juana Leal de Tarín and Concepción [Consolación] Leal de Garza,[43] who still live on their farms on the banks of the San Antonio River, were among those innocent and unfortunate prisoners of La Quinta. They endured their outrageous captivity with spirited courage before yielding to the shameful proposals of their jailers.

After the battle of Medina, Colonel Elizondo left San Antonio with five hundred men in pursuit of the fugitives, who were on the road to the United States. At the Trinity

La Quinta. After his victory over the insurgents in August 1813, Spanish general Joaquín de Arredondo converted this structure into a prison for San Antonio women. Navarro details how the women were forced to grind corn on *metates* to feed Arredondo's army and how they heroically endured many indignities and abuses. Morgan Wolfe Merrick drew this sketch of La Quinta, ca. 1855. Courtesy Daughters of Republic of Texas Library, San Antonio.

River on the old road from San Antonio he overtook a body of men and families, and at that point one hundred five persons were shot.

Perhaps I shall be accused of exaggerating by giving a historical account of the method of judgment by which those captured on the Trinity were condemned and executed.

Elizondo had for a chaplain a despicable priest known as Padre Camacho.[44] When some of the fugitive insurgents were captured, Elizondo brought them to the confessional and ordered this clergyman to confess them according to the rites of the Catholic Church. Christian sentiment and hope of eternity compelled those unfortunate men to confess truthfully, without reserve, the part they had taken in the revolution. Padre Camacho, with the proof of these confessions, would give a prearranged signal to the officers of the guard so that they might lead the victim immediately to the place of execution.

Another aggravating circumstance may fill the readers with horror. Padre Camacho had been a casualty at the battle of Alazán, wounded by a spent bullet[45] which broke the muscles of his leg. More than once on the Trinity River, when some wretch condemned to death pleaded aloud for mercy, the priest, raising his clerical habit would say to him, "Move on my son and suffer the penalty in the name of God, because the ball that wounded me may have come from your rifle."

After these executions on the Trinity River, Elizondo returned with all the afflicted families as prisoners,[46] among whom were many black-eyed and beautiful women. He invited the weaker sex to bathe their delicate forms while they were being compelled, with hands tied, to cross the San Antonio River on foot at the very place now occupied by the pleasant bath house of Mr. Hall.

Who could have foretold that the heads of the famous spies of General Gutiérrez, Culás, Botas Negras and Ayamontes, whom Arredondo had executed in San Antonio, would be caged and placed on the point of a pike at the same place where the American banner now proudly waves on Military Plaza?[47] Who could have foretold that thirty-three years after this emblem of terror was flaunted by tyrants to instill fear, that a flag respected by the world would mark the place where those lifeless heads had been exhibited?

After Mexican Independence was won, Governor Trespalacios crossed the Medina River on his way to San

Antonio and, upon viewing the prairies sprinkled with human skeletons,[48] had them collected and buried with military honors. I distinctly remember the following inscription written on a square of wood which was on the trunk of an oak tree:

> Here lie the brave Mexicans,
> Following the example of Leonidas,
> Who sacrificed their wealth and lives
> Fighting ceaselessly against tyrants.

This is an imperfect but truthful history of the events of that period.

After the arrival of Arredondo, San Antonio remained quiet and subject to the dominion of the king of Spain. He confiscated and sold the property of the patriots—known as rebels—who never recovered their belongings, not even after the consummation of Mexican independence in the year of 1821.

The noble citizens of Béxar sacrificed their lives and property, performing heroic deeds of valor in the year 1813. Yet they left to their descendants no other inheritance than the indifference and ingratitude of the Mexican Republic.

They never received any compensation or indemnity, not even the due respect and gratitude from their fellow citizens of Mexico. Our courage and heroism were cast into oblivion by the government of that ancient and renowned land. For that reason, I do not believe that anyone will be surprised by the germ of discontent that the people of Texas harbored. For this reason they adhere to the new order of things that is offered to us by the institutions of a great, powerful and appreciative republic. Such is the beginning that brought about the Independence of Texas, which separated itself from that government forever.

Perhaps this subject can be continued at a later date. October 30, 1853.

San Geronimo Ranch House.
Purchased in 1834, the Navarros' eighty-eight hundred acre ranch on the Tio Geronimo Creek (hence the name) was their primary residence from ca. 1840 through 1853. The Navarros also maintained a residence in San Antonio. José Antonio wrote much of his correspondence from the ranch and probably wrote the 1853 installment of *Apuntes* there. Although no longer extant, the ranch was located about seven miles north of Seguin, Texas. This photo was taken ca. 1930s. Courtesy Carol Bading and Leon Studio, Seguin, Texas.

José Antonio Navarro wrote this letter to Oscar Keeler from his
San Geronimo Ranch on February 15, 1853. This document reflects
the eloquent Spanish of Navarro's correspondence and other
writings. Courtesy David McDonald.

San Antonio Ledger, 1857-1858

*Navarro published three installments of historical commentaries
in the* San Antonio Ledger *during 1857-1858. As in his earlier
1853 work, these commentaries were directed at an
Anglo-American readership and were translated into English.
This effort was Navarro's response to Henderson Yoakum's*
History of Texas *(1855). Subsequently, Navarro's original
Spanish version appeared in the 1869 compilation entitled*
Apuntes Históricos Interesantes de San Antonio de Béxar.

Commentaries of Historical Interest

To the editor of the *Ledger*: [PRINTED 12 DECEMBER 1857]

In numbers 27 and 28 of the month of December 1853[49]
of this newspaper, the author of these notes wrote about the
invasion of General Bernardo Gutiérrez and other events
occurring in 1812 and 1813. It was Gutiérrez who brought
from the United States those six hundred or more North
Americans and volunteers, intrepid auxiliaries of Mexican
independence. They fought more than ten months against the
troops of the king of Spain at the walls of Goliad and on the
fields of the Rosillo and Alazán. The insurgents finally suc-
cumbed in the bloody battle of Medina on the 18th of August,
1813, defeated by the superior force brought by veteran
Spanish General Joaquín de Arredondo from the interior of
Mexico.

It seems that this history would be of no little interest for
your readers, especially for the present residents of Goliad,
San Antonio, and the surrounding area, where their delightful
meadows and crystalline springs were splattered with the

ee

blood of defenders of liberty that was spilled many years ago. It would seem to be of no little interest to read and understand now, through the mouth of an eyewitness, about the origin of the many conflicts in which the heroic native scions of San Antonio took an active part beginning in the year 1811.

I write this booklet as an inveterate devotee to historical materials, without literary pretensions, against all mercenary purposes, and feeling myself free and above those who do such for profit. The events I narrate were fixed in my retina at the time they occurred, and I have no need to resort to periphrases or allegories, as in mythological accounts.

Paper, pen and ink, and an ardent desire that some able and conscientious future historian will have the materials to enhance the history of this my beloved land, have caused me to write this which is, without pecuniary return, the basis of my moral ambition.

The public will have seen the history of Texas written by the deceased Yoakum.[50] While in many respects the work is appreciable and precise, it is plagued by a number of inexactitudes, such as this example: having Governor Antonio Cordero among the fourteen Spanish officials dying on the Rosillo by having his throat cut. It is certain that Cordero lived at least until 1821 in Mexico.[51] Likewise, Yoakum says that the father of Captain Antonio Delgado[52] was shot in San Antonio and his head put on public display—yet we know well that the venerable man died of old age and sorrow at the Trinity River while Elizondo was pursuing the fugitives from the battle of Medina.

In this manner, Colonel Yoakum falls into other small errors which, although they do not damage the substance of his history, do impart an inconceivable inconstancy, such as when he says: *that because of wars with the Indians, the troops of the Alamo were compelled* [italics in original] during the year

1785 to remain within the walls of the mission. It is true that this happened, but it occurred when these troops were at Alamo de Parras in Mexico, long before they came to this Valero mission—which was called by that name since its foundation. It only took on the name "Alamo" after the troops of Alamo de Parras came to the Valero Mission, which was during the years of 1803 to 1804, and they remained at this mission continuously until the revolution of [1813].[53]

These motives and the urging of some of my friends, who have desired to know about the most important contemporaneous events that happened in our city, have persuaded me to write this brief chronicle.

I do not write for the heartless nor for the egoists—to whom the glories and misfortunes of men of another origin and language matter little or not at all. I write for the humanitarian and cultured who understand how to respect and empathize with the tribulations of a valiant people who have struggled in the midst of their own ignorance guided only by an instinct for their liberty, against enemies so superior that they may be placed alongside the most free and fortunate nations of all mankind—such as the nation with the flag of stars. I write in order to inform our Americans, however indignant some of them among us may be, who with base, aggressive pretexts want to uproot from this classic land its legitimate people who are the descendants of those who fifty years ago spilled their blood searching for the liberty of which we now vaingloriously boast.

Beginning with the years 1807 and 1808, when it appeared that the Spanish nation was breathing its last gasps as a result of the invasion by that prodigious conquistador, Napoleon I, Mexicans began quietly planning to shake off the ominous yoke of the mother country. Not because it was dismembered and nearly absorbed by the formidable conquistador, but because they could no longer tolerate the swarms of petty Spanish tyrants. These, in their angry impotence, in their frenetic delirium which caused the ruptures in the Spanish peninsula, inflicted unimaginable cruelties on the peaceful scions of Mexico, accompanied with violent pecuniary extortion in order to divide the booty among the tumultuous juntas and governments which were the provincial governments of Spain.

Never have people of the land seen a mosaic more confusingly inlaid with orders and decrees, all intended for the oppression and plunder of the unfortunate Mexican people.

On the 8th of September, 1808, a French General named Octaviano D'Alvimar arrived in San Antonio.[54] It was said he had traveled incognito through the United States and entered Texas through Nacogdoches. It was precisely D'Alvimar whom Napoleon had sent as the proclaimed viceroy of Mexico.

We saw him enter the plaza of San Antonio with his flamboyant uniform. Covered with insignia and brilliant crosses, it challenged the amiable sun—which nevertheless continued to illuminate the plaza of San Antonio until its decline in the west. But it appears that General D'Alvimar was yet unaware of the reverses in fortune of his master the emperor, and that the arrogant and indomitable Spanish people were struggling through rivers of blood to throw off French domination. He was unaware that astute inquisitorial orders, peculiar to Spanish diplomacy in emergent transactions, were now anticipated by the viceroyalty to the end that D'Alvimar be taken prisoner and sent under guard to the capital of Mexico. This was the determination of Antonio Cordero, governor of the province. It appears that this incident was accompanied by Spanish triumphs on the Peninsula and more terror for the conspirators' activities in America, but nevertheless the Mexicans continued their secret conspiracies to win independence from their colonial rulers.

On the other hand, reports that were arriving from the Peninsula each day were gloomy and alarming. The troops of Napoleon triumphed everywhere and thousands of Spaniards were swearing obedience to the French emperor. Finally it was learned that a French magistrate, sent by Napoleon, would soon come to receive and take charge of the Viceroyalty of Mexico.

The priest of the town of Dolores, Miguel Hidalgo, was one of the conspirators. The shout for independence[55] was prepared for a certain day, but a Mexican [Benedict] Arnold entrusted with the secret gave the warning the Viceroy of Mexico had anticipated. The priest Hidalgo gave the shout at midnight of the sixteenth of September—even a delay of two hours probably would have seen him a prisoner on the way to Mexico, with all hope of independence dashed.

¡*Viva Nuestra Señora de Guadalupe*; *and mueran los Gachupines!*[56] This was the first invocation that occurred to him in those portentous moments. Upon such fragile auspices a revolution of fruitful results was born that has raised a federal republic that is a member of the family of nations.

Let those who judge these anomalies with astonishment pause and contemplate the times and the capacities of the people there. Let them put themselves in the place of the patriot Hidalgo, already denounced as a traitor before the implacable despot, the Viceroy of Mexico.[57] Imagine being in a pressing situation without the slightest plan of operation, without money, arms, or troops, having no more than a few hundred Indians from his own village. Neither the rigorous mind of a Washington nor the iron will of a Napoleon I could have led these chaotic, backward masses to so great an enterprise without motivating them by means of vengeance and superstition, just as this illustrious and unfortunate patriot was compelled to do.

The plunder and slaughter, a necessary consequence, began at that point. But how powerful are the instincts of a people who fight for a just cause! The Mexicans, in the midst of those inevitable disorders, triumphed everywhere by the end of 1810.

All across the kingdom the people arose in mass, expelling, imprisoning and putting Spaniards to the sword. The echoes of the insurgent triumphs were heard into all the most remote provinces and this day arrived in San Antonio de Béxar.

A garrison of two thousand soldiers of the king covered this city and military points across to the Sabine River, their principal orders being to guard the Province of Texas at all hazards against initiatives by the United States. Here the officials and troops were more clever than those of Nuevo León and Nuevo Santander. Each soldier, one could say, was a citizen-capitalist—a distinguished calling to which the Viceroy of Mexico was passionately devoted. Is it surprising that at this time San Antonio was at the height of its prosperity? Hundreds of thousands in gold and silver coin came into the city every two months for the diligent maintenance of the troops. It was a common sight to see a soldier expend a hundred pesos on a meal—[58] and with the same nonchalance with which today we invite a friend to have a glass of beer.

[*SAN ANTONIO LEDGER*, 19 DECEMBER 1857]

Despite all these individual pleasures that were being enjoyed, the life of a great people is rooted in the totality of human society. The citizens and troops of San Antonio began to manifest some anxiety about the political fortune of Mexico, and rumors and accusations against the Spanish governors now were noted in conversations among friends.

The descendants of the first Islanders, the settlers of Béxar, its legitimate original masters, found bold and daring ways to humiliate the arrogance of the Spanish governors. The Delgados, Arochas, Leales, Traviesos and others[59] had established privileged families in Béxar that were considered nobility from the time their fathers sailed from the Canary Islands to settle in the Province of Texas in the year 1730.

Here their well honed pride and zealous indignation against the despotic actions of the Spanish governors germinated. There could have been no opportunity more suitable for these belligerent nobles than the one provided by the reports from Mexico regarding the triumphs gained by the priest Hidalgo and the other leaders of the insurrection.

There was, nevertheless, considerable resistance to declaring a military rebellion. The principal military leaders were of Spanish origin. There were others of Mexican origin, but they restrained themselves with respectful delicacy from initiating the first rebellion against the rights of the monarchy that had ruled for three hundred years.

To avoid this conflict of interest, the citizens chose individuals from the army who were neither officials of high rank (for the delicacy of the situation would make them useless for the enterprise), nor simple soldiers whose awareness of their inferiority would compel them to waver in the hour of danger.

Thus three sergeants were selected to seduce the army: Miguel Reyna, Blas José Perales and Trinidad Pérez. They put all the troops under arms in the barracks that were located in La Villita,[60] to the east of San Antonio.

At dawn on January 22, 1811, they offered command of this army to the militia captain of Nuevo Santander, Juan Bautista Casas, who accepted and put himself at the head of fifteen hundred men.

Casas marched in columns toward the plaza of government.[61] Accompaning him as representatives of the citizens were Gavino Delgado, Francisco Travieso and Vicente Flores. Dawn was just beginning to break when the battalions, now in closed column, faced the plaza of government.

Captain Casas, as ranking officer, entered and made prisoners of the Governors Salcedo, Herrera and other Spanish officials, who still slept the placid sleep of twilight, confident that no one would move against their omnipotent persons.

This memorable day of January 22, 1811, was the first occasion in which the Mexicans of San Antonio de Béxar announced their desire to break forever the chains of their ancient colonial slavery.

This was the day in which they no longer attempted to restrain the trembling, guttural voice that pervades the long and servile life, and they were able to speak out loudly to those who had been the absolute masters of the Mexicans. But the sudden transformation of that day, in which the slaves were elevated to masters and the arbiters of their oppressors and masters of yesterday, generated a bitter vanguard directed against those called *gachupines*.

Captain Casas hastened to send the fourteen Spanish officers, well laden with chains, to the interior of Mexico.

The sixteenth of February of the same year a formidable guard, commanded by the same Don Vicente Flores and sergeant Miguel Reyna, set out from Béxar with orders to deliver the prisoners to the insurgent Brigadier Pedro Aranda, who was at the Presidio del Rio Grande.[62]

Everything seemed to indicate the sure triumph of Mexican independence, and there was scarcely anyone who did not envy the glory of those who had dared to put the Spanish oppressors in chains.

But human nature being what it is today, the more vehement the outbursts of the courageous spirit, the more fleeting its duration may be. Very few days passed before ominous signs appeared that were badly disguised—like the sick person who affects not to know the gravity of his illness in order to deny the approaching end of his existence. No omens could have signified more tragedy than those of January 22.

Casas and the other Coryphaeus[63] feigning not to recognize the pervasive danger, freely permitted the masses of the town and the troops of the garrison to discuss the news that was arriving from Mexico, news which exaggerated the setbacks suffered by the priest Hidalgo and which painted a desperate situation for the armies of independence.

It was unfortunately the truth! The glories of Hidalgo, Allende, Abasolo and other illustrious captains of independence had been eclipsed near the capital of Mexico and, with their defeated army, they were in retreat toward the provinces of Coahuila and Texas. They were hauling more than five million [pesos] in gold and silver coin with the goal of reaching the United States and raising a large army of American volunteers.

What inscrutable judgments of Providence on high! What mortal man dares to question its divine dispositions? But permit us, brazen in our filial sentiment, to ask: why did You not permit those unfortunate heroes and their rich cargo to reach the classic land of the United States of the North, thus avoiding those ten years of cruel war in which more than five hundred thousand Mexicans disappeared, dead on the battlefield and by execution? . . . But let us throw a respectful veil over mysteries that should not be exposed by human reason and continue with the events that took place in San Antonio de Béxar.

Captain Juan Bautista Casas was a native of San Fernando

in the old province of Nuevo Santander. He was a member of the militia company of Croix and still was when he died at the age of thirty-six years.[64] A capitalist in his country, he nevertheless served the military calling with honor, and his talents while moderate were disinterested and honorable. He accepted the command offered by the citizens and the military garrison of San Antonio because he believed that the time had arrived to fight the natural enemies of his country, and because above all he was a man of the type whose excessive urbanity made him incapable of resisting overtures and importunity.

This is the man placed at the head of that revolutionary volcano which burst forth from a people without a war strategy, without political principles, and with no guide other than the blind impulse for vengeance. These discordant elements enabled the Spaniards to introduce their emissaries and proclamations, with which they easily manipulated the revolutionary spirit into what was called the counter-revolution— the return to the obedience of the tyrant-king of Spain.

Father Juan Manual Zambrano, a native of Béxar, was designated to effect the counter-revolution in favor of the Spaniards. Gigantic and obese, arrogant in manner, dynamic and volatile as mercury, he possessed a special talent for total disorder.[65]

It is not my intention to rebuke the conduct of those who took part in this counter-revolution that hastened the unfortunate Casas to the execution block, but rather to deplore and pity the errant reasoning of those who, imbued with the false honor of being faithful to the most detestable tyrant of Europe, made an ostentatious show of plunging the fratricidal dagger into the heart of their Mexican brothers. Thus they hammered the rivets of their own chains, condemning themselves to trudge sorrowfully behind the plodding Spanish ox to earn their daily bread.

On March 3, 1811, Juan Bautista Casas was surprised and taken prisoner by the said priest, Juan Manuel Zambrano, in the same government offices where, thirty-nine days before, he had imprisoned the governors with the aid of these same troops. Casas surrendered with the serenity of a courageous man. But upon seeing himself surrounded by bayonets of the same men who a few days ago had been his friends and conspirators, he spoke to them in anger: "Are you the same individuals who placed me in this office and now you must add infamy to treason by capturing me and delivering me to the execution block?"

"Silence, wretched traitor," replied one of his captors with the same fanatical and wordy judgments used by the inquisitors when they were going to burn the so-called heretics on a pile of green wood in the holy name of God. "Silence, and submit to the justice and mercy of our most beloved sovereign, our Lord, Fernando VII. Long live the king!" At this thunderous shout the bells began ringing continuously, the cheers from the troops and the people altogether created a pharisaic bedlam, like savage cannibals surrounding the victim they are about to sacrifice. Then it was announced that the unfortunate Captain Casas was in chains, and the inhabitants of San Antonio returned to the status of vassals of the king of Spain.

[*SAN ANTONIO LEDGER*, 2 JANUARY 1858]

Let us leave poor Casas, groaning in his chains within a filthy and lonely prison cell, and survey what was happening at this time on the other side of the Rio Grande.

We have already said that, since February 16, Governors Salcedo, Herrera, and other officers had been confined in prison—making a total of fourteen prisoners. Upon their arrival in Monclova, the Mexican Colonel Ignacio Elizondo declared in favor of the king, and Salcedo, Herrera, and the officers were set at liberty. Together, they plotted with cunning schemes the surest way to lure the priest Hidalgo with his army, which was still in the city of Saltillo, in order to take him prisoner by means of deception. If successful, it would follow as a matter of course that all the provinces of Northern Mexico would, one after the other, declare for the king's cause.

President Zambrano foresaw all this from Béxar and with cunning revolutionary strategy immediately dispatched two spies, Captains José Muñoz and Luis Galán. They set out March 8, with adequate double instructions to be utilized in the event that they should encounter the priest Hidalgo or the generals of the king—for the idea was to be well received if stopped by either of the belligerent parties.

It inspires compassion rather than horror to contemplate the bewildering entanglements to which the Machiavellian education of the superior Spanish leaders had led the unwary Mexicans. They encouraged among them the most contemptible deeds of weak wills and of treason with the base purpose of destroying every generous impulse in their bosoms, converting them into wretched instruments of their own destruction.

Upon arrival in Monclova, Muñoz and Galán saw that everyone was already disposed in favor of the king. They told the Spanish governors the agreeable news that the traitor Casas was imprisoned in Béxar and relayed the congratulations of the faithful vassals of His Majesty from all of Texas.

Immediately they dispatched an express courier to inform President Zambrano of the happy result of his diplomatic mission and at the same time requested that he send the prisoner Casas to Monclova as soon as possible, where he was to await trial for the crimes he had committed against the king. But Zambrano was now a consummate master of intrigue, more so than his Spanish teachers, and he delayed sending Casas until having assured himself of the state of affairs in the interior of Mexico.

When he received a reliable report about the well-organized plan in Monclova by which the entire army of the priest Hidalgo would without doubt be made prisoner, Zambrano transferred the illustrious captive on the 2nd of July, 1811, under a guard headed by the sergeant of La Bahía , Juan José Calderón.

Zambrano also departed on the 26th of the same month. Accompanied by his government junta and all the troops of San Antonio, he advanced to the city of Laredo.

Casas arrived at Monclova around the middle of July. Cordero and the other Spanish governors were there. Monclova was the focus for all the illustrious Castilians, and how they looked forward to Sicilian vespers[66] for the unfortunate Hidalgo.

Casas faced criminal charges before a military council of war, of which Cordero was president, and was unanimously condemned to face the firing squad. When the prosecutor read the death sentence Casas knelt, listened to it, and then according to custom kissed that paper containing the fatal message.

Poor Casas! He was a traditional and sincere Christian. When he was asked if he had anything to say concerning his sentence, he replied, "No! because I know that I have failed my sovereign. I wish only one favor of his royal clemency, and that is that a small portion from the sale of my property be given for the support of my poor aged mother during her few remaining days. The royal treasures of His Majesty are enormous and it would not affect them in the slightest degree if a small sum were deducted from my own estate. Likewise, I would request that two hundred pesos which I owe be paid which I am in no position to pay if you confiscate all my property after my death. I have nothing more to ask."

As it was already known that the army of the priest Hidalgo was due to arrive at Acatita de Baján, the execution of Casas was postponed. On July 27, the priest Hidalgo was made prisoner with thirty-two generals, his entire staff, two thousand soldiers, and a little more than three and one-half million pesos in gold and silver coin. Everything fell into the hands of Elizondo and the governors.

Hidalgo and most of the generals were taken to Chihuahua and were shot. After this event, that is to say, on August 1, Casas was placed in the death cell, and on August 3 he was executed in Monclova at the foot of Zapopa Hill. His head was ordered to be cut off and sent to San Antonio. Although it arrived in only three and one-half days, the head had already decayed and it was necessary to bury it.

General Bernardo Gutiérrez, then a colonel in the army of Hidalgo, upon learning what had happened July 27, became a fugitive. After traveling through the deserts of Texas, he arrived in the United States from whence he brought the American volunteers for the campaign of 1812 and 1813.

We have seen the ephemeral duration of Mexican Independence in Texas in 1811, the tragic end of Casas, and how all hopes of liberty were extinguished. Thus the Spanish governors returned from Monclova to assume their former positions of command. President Zambrano and the government junta delivered the command over to the officials of the king. The people of San Antonio returned to their limited options of blindly obeying one king of Heaven, another of the earth, and laboring to earn their daily bread.

If we contemplate this complacent conformity, of an untutored community which entrusted its entire ambition and both its worldly and eternal happiness to the pleasing of both a celestial and terrestrial sovereign, the question naturally arises: Would it not be better for the human race to reduce its thought and obligations to the obedience of only two superior agents *(although it may be supposed they are not flawless) before meddling in the bitter and difficult struggle of trying to examine, comprehend, and handle all the links of the intricate machinery of a government?*

Is it better for the health of the body and tranquility of the spirit to live in passive ignorance of the powers of mankind and of their rulers in order to avoid facing the armies of the villains of the world? . . .

[text missing] some of which prevail by brutal force while dressed in the vestments of liberty and equality, while others rob and kill poor people and many times vilify the same persons who have given them a country and power? [67]

But even if such complacent peace resulting from blind obedience were to be desired, new aspirations were already entering the impetuous hearts of the noble Islanders, transmitted from the neighbor republic to the north, across the seas and through the narrow trails of what then were the unsettled lands of Texas.

The appeal of ideas and customs from beyond the mountains faded before the incomparable satisfaction of a people-king in the Americas; the tottering Spanish rulers would very soon be broken apart by the moral strength of republican institutions. These noble Islanders harbored such ideas, but acted on them much later and then with no more success than to bring ruin upon themselves and to be nearly exterminated from the land which had given them birth and which their forefathers had conquered.

In November of 1812, barely sixteen months after the catastrophe of Acatita de Baján, Bernardo Gutiérrez entered Texas. With that little army of Leonidas[68] North Americans he took La Bahía and later San Antonio, on April 1, 1812.

Immediately the Delgados, Arochas, Traviesos, Leales, and many others, recalling how much they had suffered the previous year for the cause of independence, joined Gutiérrez and his army, body and soul.

They fought with passion and zeal against the might of the terrible Arredondo. But Arredondo triumphed in the famous battle of Medina, and these patriots lay dead in the fields of battle and at the places of execution. A few emigrated to the United States never to return. These courageous souls lost everything.

Mexican independence, germinated in the blood of these martyrs, was finally declared in September 1821.

But what ingratitude! Not one single murmur ever crossed the mountains of Anahuac [Mexico City] to console the broken remnant of those brave patriots. Such is the end for heroes! Perhaps their renown would be more complete if they were to receive the miserable compensation due from their fellow men. To complete the picture of misfortune, the few descendants who survive in San Antonio are disappearing, murdered in full view of a people who boast of their justice and excellence.

Consolación Leal,[69] heroine of those days, died a few months ago, killed by a Spaniard, and Antonio Delgado[70] was riddled by bullets from the rifle of an American bastard.

May Divine Providence use these historical commentaries to stir generous hearts to treat with more respect this race of men who, as the legitimate proprietors of this land, lost it together with their lives and their hopes, to follow in the footsteps of those very ones who now enjoy the land in the midst of peace and plenty.

After the 1853 sale of San Geronimo Ranch, the Navarros improved their San Antonio home site by building this new house—"Casa Navarro." Completed by 1856, this house became José Antonio's primary residence—although he spent a great deal of time at his Atascosa Ranch about thirty miles south of San Antonio. Navarro also owned the two-story building next to the house, which he rented out as a store in the 1860s. These are two of the three structures which today form the Casa Navarro State Historical Park, San Antonio. Courtesy David McDonald.

Antebellum table on display at Casa Navarro State Historical Park, San Antonio. Contemporaries of Navarro observed that his furnishings demonstrated his unpretentious lifestyle. Courtesy David McDonald.

Interior view of Casa Navarro State Historical Park, San Antonio.
Courtesy David McDonald.

José Antonio Navarro Bicentennial Statue by sculptor Jonas Perkins.
Courtesy David McDonald.

Endnotes

[1]"Colonel" is used here as a title of respect for a prominent man. Navarro never served in a military capacity, evidently because of a lame leg that was broken in childhood. See note 8 below.

[2]Numerous San Antonio newspapers in Spanish, often dedicated to a particular cause or point of view, came and went during this period such as the *Bejareño, Ranchero, Correo, Mexicano de Texas,* and *Atalaya de Texas.* Evidently, Leal first published the commentaries in one of these without Navarro's permission.

[3]Abbreviation for "Que Besan Sus Manos", who kiss your hands. A standard concluding phrase in Spanish and Mexican correspondence.

[4]Narciso Leal. For a brief biographical treatment of N. Leal see note 2 on page 27.

[5]Angel Navarro was born in Ajaccio, Corsica, ca. 1749. In a 1792 autobiographical sketch, he said he ran away from home at age thirteen or fourteen and left Corsica in 1762. Despite subsequent reports that he came to colonial Mexico as a Spanish military officer, or in other high office, his origins were more humble. After leaving Corsica, he worked as a servant in Genoa, Barcelona, and Cádiz. From Cádiz he came to colonial Mexico as a servant and learned the merchant trade in the province of Nuevo León. By 1779 he had arrived in San Antonio, where he was listed as a twenty-seven year old unmarried merchant, having the property of one horse. Angel Navarro's autobiographical sketch dated 14 May 1792 is in the Béxar Archives Microfilm, Roll 70, 323; also see 1779 Béxar Census entitled *"Estado Gral de la Tropa de el Pres[idio[de S.n Ant[onio] de Béxar y Vecind[ario] de la Villa de S.n Fernando . . .1.°, 2.° 3.° del mes de Julio de 1779,"* Archivo General de Indias, Guadalajara legajo 283, Sevilla, Spain.

[6]Josefa Ruiz was born in San Antonio 22 November 1766. Her parents were Juan Manuel Ruiz, of Querétaro; and Manuela de la Peña of Saltillo. *San Fernando Church Confirmations 1759, and Baptismals, Book 1,1731-1774 ,* #205, page 13 of baptismal records.

[7]The earliest published biographical sketch of Navarro states

that he was sent "to one of the best schools in Saltillo, at age ten, where he remained for a few years" and that he subsequently educated himself through reading and the study of law. J[acob] de Cordova, *Texas: Her Resources and Her Public Men . A Companion for J. De Cordova's New and Correct Map of the State of Texas* (Philadelphia: J.B. Lippincott, 1858), 146.

[8]The accident probably occurred around 1808. Writing to Santa Anna ca. 1843, Navarro reportedly said he broke his leg more that thirty-five years earlier. Bancroft Papers, 1023, cited in Noel M. Loomis, *The Texan-Santa Fe Pioneers* (Norman: University of Oklahoma Press, 1958), 26

[9]The text says "September 17." Navarro was either mistaken about or misquoted this date, since the *Ledger's* publishing schedule did not include the seventeenth. Navarro was evidently responding to the *Ledger* of 15 September 1853, which included a contemptuous account of Texas history.

[10]An ironic understatement of the arrogant opinions expressed in the *Ledger* article of September 15.

[11]A town in Michoacán where the first Mexican Constitution was published in 1814.

[12]Present Nuevo Guerrero, a town in Mexico located about ten miles north of Mier.

[13]Since Nacogdoches is not on the Trinity, Navarro is probably referring to Trinidad de Salcedo, a settlement and military post founded in 1805 near the intersection of the Trinity River and the road to Nacogdoches.

[14]The last Spanish governor of Texas, 1808-1813.

[15]Simón de Herrera, a native of the Canary Islands, was governor of the province of Nuevo Leon. Commandant Nemesio de Salcedo ordered him to Texas in 1806 to bolster the defense of the eastern frontier of Texas against French and North American intrusions. He eventually took an active role, along with Governor Salcedo, as an administrator of Spanish Texas. Félix D. Almaraz, *Tragic Cavalier: Manuel Salcedo of Texas, 1808-1813*, (Austin: University of Texas Press, 1971), 30-34.

[16]José Bernardo Maxmiliano Gutiérrez de Lara was a merchant,

blacksmith, and land owner from the state of Tamaulipas, Mexico. After the capture of Hidalgo and other revolutionary leaders in 1812, he was authorized by rebels to seek aid in the United States. He went to Washington, D.C., where he discussed his plans for revolution in Texas with Secretary of State James Monroe. On his return to Louisiana, Gutiérrez recruited as officers in his army: Augustus William Magee of Boston, Samuel Kemper from Virgina, Henry Perry of Connecticut, and Ruben Ross, a native of Virgina.

[17]The Rosillo (or Rosalis) was a prairie near the junction of Salado Creek and the San Antonio River located southeast of San Antonio. *Handbook of Texas*, II: 502

[18]*labor* was an area of cultivated fields, or a single field. A *labor* also had a precise designation: 177.1 acres of farm land. The lower *labor* Navarro refers to was located south of San Antonio, and was irrigated from the main *acequia* (ditch).

[19]Literally "Royal Houses." Located on the east side of Main Plaza, opposite San Fernando Church, the Casas Reales was in effect a royal courthouse, the seat of colonial government that included a jail and evidently the governors' residence.

[20]Native San Antonian José María Rodríguez, in his memoirs, describes Mariano Rodríguez as a distant relative. Omitting any reference to the 1811 revolution and junta, Rodríguez describes Mariano Rodríguez as a military man who was in charge of the Mexican forces in San Antonio during the Texas Revolution. He fought in the battle of San Jacinto (21 April 1836), then moved to Mexico. He returned to San Antonio after 1848 and died at the beginning of the Civil War. J[osé] M[aría] Rodríguez, *Rodríguez Memoirs of Early Texas* (San Antonio: Passing Show Printing, 1913; reprint, San Antonio: Standard, 1961), 53.

[21]"*Velduque (or Belduque)*" is a large sharp-pointed knife imported from Bois-le-Duc (Holland), from whence the names: "*Bolduque* and *Belduque*."

[22]Only thirteen victims are listed here. Citing Navarro as a source, Henderson Yoakum named fourteen victims in his 1855 *History of Texas from Its First Settlement in 1685 to Its Annexation to the United States in 1846* (New York: Redfield, 1855; reprint, Austin: Steck, 1935), 1:169. Yoakum's lists states: "*Spaniards*: Manuel de Salcedo, governor; Simón de Herrera, governor of New León;

Geronimo Herrera, lieutenant-colonel; Juan de Echeverría, captain; José Groscochia, captain; Francisco Pereira, captain; José Mateos, captain; Juan Ignatio Arambido, captain; Gregoria [sic] Amado, lieutenant; Antonio Lopez, citizen. Mexicans: Miguel de Areos, captain; Luis, his son, lieutenant; Francisco, his son, ensign [not listed by Navarro]; Juan Caso, lieutenant."

[23]Not "decapitated," as degollado is often rendered. "The Historical Notes" taken from John Villars, a survivor of the battle of Medina, said Salcedo and his men were taken to Rosillo Creek to "have their throats cut." The Papers of Mirabeau Buonaparte Lamar, ed. Charles Adams Gulick, Jr. and Katherine Elliott (Austin: Von Boeckmann-Jones, 1973), 6:151. Father J. M. Rodríguez recorded that, as a favor, Salcedo was shot, "Notes de Cure Dn. J. M. Rodríguez sur l'invasion des insurges du Texas l'annee 1812 et delle de 1813," Jean Louis Berlandier papers, Henry Raup Wagner Collection, University of Texas at San Antonio Library, Special Collections.

[24]Juan Martín de Echavarría was appointed Lieutenant Governor and Commander of Béxar during the rebel uprising. (Adán Benavides, Jr., ed. and comp., The Béxar Archives 1717-1836: A Name Guide (Austin: University of Texas Press, 1989), 284.

[25]On August 28, 1813, Father José Dario Zambrano interred the remains of the officers in San Fernando Church—including Joaquín de Ugarte, a fifteenth officer not listed by Navarro. San Fernando Cathedral Deaths, 28 August 1813, CASA; Frederick Charles Chabot, With the Makers of San Antonio. Genealogies of the Early Latin, Anglo-American, and German Families with Occasional Biographies, Each Group Being Prefaced With a Brief Historical Sketch and Illustrations, (San Antonio: Artes Graficas, 1937), 240-41.

[26]Evidently "casa de Gobierno" refers to the building or part of the Casas Reales where the normal business of government took place.

[27] Breve Apologia Que el Coronel D. José Bernardo Gutiérrez de Lara hace de las Imposturas Calumniosas Que se le Articulan en un Folleto Intitulado: Levantamiento de un General en las Tamaulipas contra la Republica o Muerto Que se le Aparece al Gobierno en Aquel Estado. Emprenta del Ciudadano Pedro Gonzalez y socio en Monterrey Año de 1827. In this work, Gutiérrez made an unsuccessful attempt to blame the emissaries of Toledo for the

murders. For a summary of this rare document, see Thomas W. Streeter, *Bibliography of Texas 1795-1845* (1955-1960), p. 242.

[28]The Presidio del Rio Grande was located at present Guerrero, Coahuila, about 20 miles down river from the town of Piedras Negras.

[29]Alazán Hill, according to Antonio Menchaca, *Memoirs*, by Antonio Menchaca with a foreword by Frederick Charles Chabot and an introduction by James P. Newcomb (San Antonio: Yanaguana Society, 1937), 15.

[30]Father J. M. Rodríguez refers to observers from the church tower watching the battle through a spyglass. "Notes de Cure Dn. J. M. Rodríguez."

[31]Louis Masicolt (also Massiot, Massicott, and Masicolt). Said to have been a French agent, he was one of two representatives of the army on the Béxar revolutionary junta, served Gutiérrez as secretary of state, and was mortally wounded in the Battle of Alazán while serving as aide to Perry. He understood three languages and appeared to be a young man of talents and good character about thirty years old. Henry P. Walker, ed, "William McLane's Narrative of the Magee-Gutiérrez Expedition, 1812-1813." *Southwestern Historical Quarterly* 66 (April 1963), 583.

[32]José Alvarez de Toledo, a Cuban, had represented Santo Domingo in the Spanish Cortes in 1810-1811. Disaffected with the royalists, he came to the United States and met Gutiérrez in Washington D.C. Planning revolution, they worked out an understanding that Alvarez de Toledo would remain in the U.S., operating in the interest of Mexican independence, while Gutiérrez would initate revolutionary activity along the northeastern frontier of New Spain. Ted Schwarz, *Forgotten Battlefield of the First Texas Revolution: the Battle of Medina, August 18, 1813*, ed. Robert H. Thonhoff (Austin: Eakin, 1985), 10.

[33]The Cortes of Cádiz was a parliament, or junta, that emerged in Cádiz, Spain, after Napoleon seized the Spanish crown in 1808. The Cortes claimed legal authority in the absence of the Spanish king, who was imprisoned by Napoleon.

[34]See note 27.

[35]Sometime after 1815, Alvarez de Toledo served Fernando VII

and was appointed ambassador to Naples. Vito Alessio Robles, *Coahuila y Tejas desde la consumación de la independencia hasta el tratado de Paz de Guadalupe Hidalgo*, (1979), Vol. 1: 659.

[36]For an extensive study of the battle of Medina and determination of where it occurred see Schwartz, *Forgotten Battlefield*.

[37]Cannon that fire a ball weighing four to eight pounds.

[38]Another contemporary account said that, to energize the flagging spirits of his men, Arredondo had the trumpeter play "La Diana," the Spanish army reveille, which disconcerted the insurgents and evidently awakened the spirits of the royalists. Father J. M. Rodríguez, "Notes de Cure Dn. J. M. Rodríguez."

[39]Navarro refers to the new courthouse, built beginning in 1851, that replaced the old *Casas Reales* building. The new structure, located at the north-west corner of Military Plaza, became known as the "Bat Cave" because thousands of these flying animals roosted there. Sylvia Ann Santos, *Courthouses of Béxar County, 1731-1978*, (San Antonio: Béxar County Historical Commission San Antonio, Texas, 1979), 2-3.

[40]Probably the Plaza House, which was located on the north side of Main Plaza.

[41]From 1848 to 1855 the San Antonio Post Office was located on Quinta Street (Dwyer Avenue), at the home of John Bowen. Cecilia Steinfeldt, *San Antonio Was: Views from the Slide Collection of Albert Steves*, Sr. (San Antonio: San Antonio Museum Association, 1978-79), 30.

[42]The word *"quinta"* normally refers to a rural community recreational building where festive gatherings would take place. The cost of constructing the building was a fifth of the individuals' produce hence the name *quinta*, or fifth.

[43]Juana Leal de Tarín and Consolación Leal de Garza (b. San Antonio, 1795) were sisters. Copy of a letter in possession of the authors, dated 24 March 1980: Robert Tarín to Bernice Strong.

[44]Probably José Manuel Camacho, a priest who was active in Béxar from 1809-1816. Father J.M. Rodríguez refers to the malevolent Capellan Camacho who went with the Elizondo and

royalist troops to the Trinity in pursuit of insurgents. There, at Camacho's signal, twenty to thirty captives at a time were shot. "Certainly he violated the sacramental seal [of confidentiality] to the detriment of many innocent people." Rodríguez, "Notes de Cure Dn. J. M. Rodríguez." A padre Camacho is mentioned by John Villars, "Historical Notes," in Gulick and Elliott, eds., *Papers of Lamar*, 6: 154. Antonio Menchaca refers to a priest named Esteban Camacho, who traveled with Elizondo to the Trinity in pursuit of insurgents, Menchacha, *Memoirs*, 18.

[45]"una bala fría", literally, a cold bullet.

[46]Elizondo died on the return trip, murdered by one of his officers. He was buried at the San Marcos River. Menchaca, *Memoirs*, p. 19. Schwarz, *Forgotten Battlefield*, 115.

[47]Father J. M. Rodríguez says that Arredondo conducted executions for many days, and that the heads of those executed were put in iron cages and left on display in the Plaza de Armas for most of the year. Rodríguez, "Notes de Cure Dn. J. M. Rodríguez."

[48]According to other contemporary witnesses, the primary battlefield was located *south* of the Medina River, as demonstrated by Jean Louis Berlandier's 1828 diary. Traveling north toward San Antonio, Berlandier encountered the battle site between the Atascosa and Medina rivers. It was still littered with human bones, although he said that Governor Félix Trespalacios buried most of the human remains in 1822. A cross was carved in the trunk of a live oak to indicate the site of the grave, a carving which was renewed from time to time by soldiers of the presidio. Stephen F. Austin's 1837 Map of Texas also shows the battleground south of the Medina rivers. Jean Louis Berlandier, *Journey to Mexico During the Years 1826 to 1834*, trans. Sheila M. Ohlendorf, Josette M. Bigelow, and Mary M. Standifer, with an introduction by C. H. Muller (Austin: Texas State Historical Association, 1980), 1:282-84. Austin's map is in Vito Alessio Robles, *Coahuila y Tejas desde la consumación de la independencia hasta el tratado de Paz de Guadalupe Hidalgo*, (México: Editorial Porrua, SA, Republica Argentina México, D. F., 1979), n.p. (between 408-409)

[49]These two issues of the *San Antonio Ledger* containing Navarro's *Commentaries* have not been located to date, despite an extensive search. As noted in the introduction, an English translation of this work was published in the San Antonio *Western*

Texan 1 December 1853, reproduced in Gulick and Elliott, eds., *Papers of Lamar,* 4 (part 2): 5-12.

[50]"*El malogrado Yoakum.*" In the sense used here, *malogrado* means to die prior to producing one's best work. Henderson Yoakum, b. Tennessee 1810, was the author of *History of Texas* (1855). He utilized Navarro's 1853 historical writing as source material and died in 1857 while Navarro was expanding his historical account. Navarro's 1857 installments were critical of Yoakum's 1855 work. Yoakum, *History of Texas,* 1:169. *Handbook of Texas* (Austin: Texas State Historical Association, 1952), 2: 945.

[51]Yoakum kept erroneous information about Governor Cordero in the text of his *History* and relegated Navarro's accurate account to a footnote. In fact, Manuel Antonio Cordero was not murdered with Salcedo in 1813, for he continued to serve as governor of Coahuila until 1817 and lived a number of years after that. Ross Phares, *The Governors of Texas* (Gretna: Pelican Publishing Co.,1976), 45.

[52]Antonio Delgado commanded the soldiers who in 1811 killed Governors Salcedo, Herrera, and the Spanish officers. After the battle of Medina, he was captured by Spanish forces and executed. Walker, Henry P. "William McLane's Narrative of the Magee-Gutiérrez Expedition, 1812-1813" *Southwestern Historical Quarterly* 66 (April 1963), 586.

[53]The publication says "1843", evidently a typographical error.

[54]An agent of Napoleon I, Octaviano D'Alvimar (or Alvimar) was sent to incite revolution in northern New Spain. Félix Almaraz, *Tragic Cavalier,* 25

[55]*Grito de Dolores.*

[56]Long live our Lady of Guadalupe and death to the Spaniards! *Gachupín* was a derogatory word for Spaniards. Derived from the Nahuatl word, *cacchopini* (cactus thorn), used by Aztec Native Americans with clear symbolism to characterize Spaniards by their large, conspicuous spurs. José María Santamaría, *Diccionario de Mexicanismos* (Méjico: Editorial Porrua, S.A. Av. Rep. Argentina, 15, segunda ediciôn, 1974), 541.

[57]Francisco Javier Venegas, viceroy of Mexico 1810-1813. Venegas was described as a military man of action and few words

who was bloody, cruel, and calculating. Assuming the viceregal office two days after Hidalgo proclaimed Mexican independence, Venegas undertook measures that led to the capture of the insurgent leadership, which he believed had crushed the rebellion. Manuel Garcia Puron, *Mexico y sus Governantes*, (México: Libreria de Manuel Porrua, S.A., tercer edición, 1964), 146-47.

[58]This would appear to be a gross exaggeration.

[59]It is beyond the scope of this work to annotate all the individuals mentioned by Navarro who were involved in the Casas Revolution and the counter-revolution. However, reference to almost all of them are in Benavides, ed. and comp., *Béxar Archives*. See also Chabot, ed., *With the Makers of San Antonio*; Chabot, ed., *Texas in 1811: The Las Casas and Sambrano Revolutions* (San Antonio: Yanaguana Society, 1941).

[60]A historical marker places the barracks on Arciniega Street, between S. Alamo and S. Presa Streets.

[61]Main Plaza. Navarro refers here to the *Casas Reales*. See note 19 above.

[62]Often referred to simply as "Rio Grande," the Presidio del Rio Grande has been described as the gateway to Texas. It was located on the south bank of the Rio Grande, at the present town of Guerrero, Coahuila, about twenty miles south of present Eagle Pass and Piedras Negras.

[63]Leaders. The coryphaeus were choirleaders of ancient Greek theater and by extension, group leaders.

[64]In his 1811 confession Casas confirms the biographical data Navarro reports, except that he says he had retired from the Croix militia as a captain. Casas' birthplace, San Fernando, is located about seventy-five miles southeast of Monterrey, Nuevo León. The town of Croix, was located about fifteen miles east of Ciudad Victoria, the capital of the state of Tamaulipas. Today the town is known as "Casas." The name was changed around 1827-1828, as was done in many instances to honor insurgents like the martyred Juan Bautista Casas. Chabot, *Texas in 1811*, 67-69; Martín Reyes Vayssade, et.al. *Cartografía Histórica de Tamaulipas*. (México: Instituto Tamalipeco, 1990), 105, 138.

[65]Juan José Manuel Vicente Zambrano, b. 1772 in San Antonio.

Often referred to as a priest, he actually was a subdeacon, a lower level of clergy. His belligerent attitude and actions are well documented. In 1803, citizens petitioned the governor to restrain his aggressive activities. Navarro's personal experience with the tempetuous Zambrano may have shaped his commentaries about him. As a twelve-year-old boy, Navarro probably witnessed the loud disagreement Zambrano provoked at the Navarro house where Zambrano arrived demanding copies of certain legal testimonies. Navarro's father, Angel Navarrro, who was the *alcalde*, refused to provide the documents without due payment. After a heated exchange, the charges and countercharges by Zambrano and the *alcalde* were placed before the Governor. Zambrano was subsequently exiled to Mexico City. However, he was able to return in 1810 and the next year organized the counter-revolution against Juan Bautista Casas. Zambrano's brother José Darío Zambrano was a priest and was pastor of the San Fernando Church from 1811-1816. Béxar Archives Microfilm Roll 36: 488-96.

[66]Synonymous with massacre. The Sicilian Vespers refers to the Easter uprising against French domination when, in 1282, Sicilians slaughtered or drove virtually all the French from Sicily.

[67]The italicized text was omitted from the *San Antonio Ledger* edition of 2 January 1858. The entire italicized text was phrased as a single question, which has been broken into three parts for clarity.

[68]Leonidas, King of Sparta, died heroically (480 B.C.) with his army of Spartans and Greeks. They were defending the pass at Thermopylae against the Persian army.

[69]Navarro angrily refers to the murder of a heroic survivor of royalist insults and abuse who was incarcerated by General Arredondo in *La Quinta*. Consolación Leal was murdered at Graytown, Texas, on May 28, 1857. Her father was Joaquín Leal, and she was married to José Leonardo de la Garza. Graytown was located on the San Antonio River, near Elmendorf, Texas, where she had a home and a ranch. [Béxar County] Probate Record Book Red "E", pp. 592-93 cited in Robert Tarín to Bernice Strong, March 24, 1990.

[70]Antonio Delgado, b. 1796 in San Antonio, was murdered in Karnes County on September 12, 1857, during the Cart War. Delgado contributed to Texas independence by fighting in the battle of Medina and in the 1835 seige of Béxar that drove General Martín

Perfecto de Cós out of Texas. Exiled in Louisiana after the royalist triumph in 1813, Delgado fought in the battle of New Orleans. The subsequent murder of this Tejano hero by North Americans enraged Navarro and provoked an investigation by the state government. *San Antonio Ledger* 19 September 1857.

APUNTES

HISTORICOS INTERESANTES

DE

San Antonio de Bexar.

Escritos por el

C. Dn. JOSE ANTONIO NAVARRO,

EN NOVIEMBRE DE 1853.

Y PUBLICADOS POR VARIOS DE SUS AMIGOS.

San Antonio de Bexar, 1869.

APUNTES
HISTORICOS INTERESANTES
DE
SAN ANTONIO DE BEXAR.

San Antonio, Junio 5 de 1869.

Al Ciudadano Coronel D. José Antonio Navarro.

Muy Sr. y amigo nuestro.

Llegados á nuestras manos por fin, los interesantes apuntes históricos escritos por V. años pasados, despues de leidos, no hemos vacilado un instante en publicarlos por la Prensa, para su mas estensa circulacion. Por tanto, suplicamos á V. que esta vez, prescindiendo de su acrisolada modestia, favoresca nuestra idea de publicar sus apuntes históricos; pues creemos firmemente que serán recibidos con júbilo por todos los ciudadanos mexicanos de Texas y principalmente por los hijos de San Antonio.

Como debemos añadir por nuestra parte, á tan importante documento, algunas aluciones análogas, no dudamos que sean insuficientes á tanto merecimiento, suplicamos á V. de nuevo, á la vez que disimule la libertad que nos tomamos de hacerlo y tome en consideracion, que mas el deseo de la publicacion de los citados interesantes apuntes de V. que la confianza de nuestros conocimientos, nos obligan á producir esos ensayos.

De V. obedientes servidores Q. B. S. M.

N. Leal y varios amigos.

San Antonio Junio 5 de 1869.

Señor Don Narciso Leal y sus amigos.

Presentes.

Muy Señores mios de mi consideracion:

He recibido la atenta carta de Vds. y enterado de su contenido, contesto diciendo:

Que desde los años de 1853 y creo 1857 escribi dos pequeños opúsculos, los cuales, por no haber en aquel tiempo prensa castellana en esta ciudad, procuré que se publicasen, traducidos en el idioma Ingles y asi vieron la luz pública.

1

Mi único objeto al escribirlos y publicarlos, fué para desvanecer algunos errores que yo habia visto publicados en la prensa americana, sobre varios episodios acaecidos en Texas, allá por los años de 1811 y 1813 que fueron tan fecundos en políticos y excitantes acontecimientos sobre la Independencia Mexicana, y donde por primera vez, los hijos de San Antonio de Bexar manifestaron su patriotismo é hicieron prodigios de valor y casi románticos tomando una parte activa los descendientes de aquellos nobles Isleños; como fueron los Delgados, Traviezos, Arochas, Leales y otra porcion de patriotas de la misma estirpe.

Por esa razon y porque siempre pensé que seria muy grato á la posteridad, saber por boca de un testigo ocular y contemporaneo, las hazañas, sacrificios y trágico fin que tubieron sus ilustres ascendientes, por solamente conseguir la Independencia y libertad Mexicana, publiqué y quedaron, desde luego al dominio público, los dichos opúsculos; por consiguiente, estan Vds en absoluta libertad de hacer di ellos el uso que les fuere placible.

No obstante, yo quedo muy reconocido á la cortesania con que gratuitamente han querido Vds. recabar la áquiescencia de ésto, vuestro muy atento servidor.que B. SS. MM.

José Antonio Navarro.

Breve rasgo biográfico sobre el autor de estos apuntes.

Pocos hombres hay que como Don José Antonio Navarro, hayan, no solo deseado ser patriotas, sino sabido serlo, que es lo que constituye ilustre al ciudadano. No trataremos de hacer aparecer al Sr Navarro como un libertador, como Bolívar, ni como un legista como Henry Clay, ni como un caudillo como Hidalgo, porque nos lo prohibe el conocimiento que tenemos de su dignidad irreprehensible, pero podemos asegurar, que su retraimiento á la vida privada, ha hecho en él mas de lo que hiciera la fama en los espaciosos salones del Senado.

Don José Antonio Navarro es uno de esos hombres que puestos en parangon con los de nota, sobresale de ellos aun con su escasa instruccion, y podemos decir, que su genio deja de parecerse al de éstos por acercarse demasiado al de B. Franklin. Todo el mundo está al tanto, más de las virtudes, que del talento de el filósofo de Filadelfia, y Don José Antonio, parece que á su ejemplo, se ha hecho acreedor al mérito que le conceden todos aquellos hombres que tienen la oportunidad de tratarlo concienzudamente. Cualquier hombre que trate al Sr. Navarro á fondo, segun las ideas de que vaya poseido ó le sugiera el humor al visitarlo, es recibido y replicado por Don José Antonio con un tacto y una cortesania que nada dejan que desear.

Los objetos y muebles que componen el menaje de sus habitaciones dan inmediatamente una idea de que este H. compatriota pertenece á ese corto número de hombres, cuyas invariables y sencillas costumbres constituyen á la vez una ciencia y un recreo, una cosa que enagena y que impone igualmente, como sí estuvieran allí en perfecta armonia, la austeridad de la ciencia, con el trato alegre y cortés de la amistad.

Ver á Don José Antonio á la edad en que escribimos estos párrafos es acordarse al instante del proloquio que dice: „tal jóven, tal viejo" porque en nada de su fisonomia cuyo tipo pertenece á la estirpe española, de nariz aguileña, ni en la pureza del color de su cara que es de un rosa encendido, ni en la uniforme blancura de su completa cabellera que adorna como un marco delgado su despejada frente, demuestra los excesos de una vejéz que haya sido prematura; al contrario, su sano juicio, el órgano comun de la inteligencia claro y pronto en percibir, su voz natural sonora y enérgica cuando la levanta y su accion fácil y acentuada, da á conocer hasta á el hombre menos observativo, que Don José Antonio Navarro se halla en la plenitud de una vejéz, cuya edad, está por decirlo así, en su primer grado de fuerza para desarrollarse con mas perfeccionada regularidad.

¡Sorprendentes efectos de una vida frugal, normada por las buenas costumbres!

Muchas veces, los mismos que escribimos estas lineas hemos tenido la dicha de pasar algunas horas al lado de ese Honorable anciano, sin atribuir mas que á tan útil y agradable compañía, la influencia en nuestra alma hácia las regiones de lo halagüeño y lo desconocido. Alejandro de Rusia decia una noche en el Teatro de Erfurth, al mismo Napoleon 1

„La amistad de un grande hombre
Es un favor de los Dioses."

Y en efecto ¡cuantas veces no habria venido á nuestra mente un pensamiento nuevo, si no hubieramos estado oyendo razonar la sana inteligencia de nuestro venerable amigo!

De seguro nos estenderiamos, si tratáramos de todos los puntos de que bien pudiera llenarse esta breve noticia para que fuera mas completa, pero satisfechos de que hay personas que probablemente deben ocuparse de la entera biografia del mismo Don José Antonio, les dejamos aquella tarea como mas competentes y mejor informados que nosotros, y solo diremos, ya para concluir, algo aunque á la ligera, sobre el nacimiento y algunas peripecias de la vida de él que nos ocupamos.

Nació Don José Antonio Navarro en esta Ciudad el 27 de Febrero en el año de 1795. Fueron sus padres Don Angel Navarro, natural de Ajaccio en Corcega (Europa) y Doña Maria Josefa Ruiz y Peña de origen español y criolla de esta Ciudad. Como un sér que parecia privilegiado por la naturaleza para las grandes y rectas ideas, bien pronto se conformó con la escasa instruccion que pudo en su tiempo recibir en el Estado de Cohahuila, pues la creyó demasiado corta para su ambicion de aprender, y fiando en la fé de formarse solo fué como Don José Antonio ha sido llamado á ocupar puestos distinguidos, primero en México, despues en la República de Texas y mas tarde en los Estados-Unidos.

La vida de Don José Antonio Navarro, puede decirse que esta dividida en tres épocas gloriosas: la de su nacimiento y juventud para Texas mexicana, á donde desde muy jóven se inició en los asuntos de la insurreccion segun los „Apuntes" que siguen. La de su edad

4

madura en que figuró notablemente en tiempo de la revolucion de Texas, republicana, en la que por la firmeza de su carácter y principios esperimentó un *desengaño* cruel, por Santa-Anna, el mas déspota de los dictadores de México: por consiguiente el resto de sus dias, desde entonces hasta la fecha, ha seguido siendo en los Estados-Unidos, el mas firme campeon de los derechos del pueblo, no obstante de vivir retirado de los asuntos públicos que se agitan hoy en el pais. Asi es como vive hoy nuestro venerable conpatriota, dando con su inflecsible conducta y hábitos arreglados las mas relevantes pruebas del buen sentido en la cuestion de los partidos políticos.

Don Jose Antonio Navarro tiene en el pais numerosos amigos de alto nombre que se complacen en recordar su mérito, no obstante la opocision de sus credos políticos.

Hay la circunstancia, de que hombres mas eminentes que él por su saber y su juventud, han brillado ante la fama de un auditorio ilustrado, pero como el relámpago y durando solo lo que dura la estacion de las lluvias, han luego desaparecido, mientras Don José Antonio siguiendo el curso de los acontecimientos ha impartido á su pátria la utilidad de su existencia acrisolada, con ese tino que solo es dado á los predestinados.

Tal es la perspectiva que observamos en la vida de este H. é interesante anciano, y á los 74 años de su edad, á la que parece que el aumento del tiempo, solo pesa sobre él para influenciar la memoria maravillosa que poseé. La lesion de su pierna izquierda contraida por un accidente en el año, motivó su tension, despnes del sufrimiento de un tumor que le provino de aquella causa.

Sin embargo, este efecto no ha impedido que nuestro venerable conciudadano ande con naturalidad y regular ejercicio.

Concluiremos este artículo, cuyo objeto es marcar con nuestro modo de sentir el carácter del autor de los „apuntes historicos" que tenemos el gusto de presentar nuestros conciudadanos como una prebenda historia del pasado de la pátria, sintiendo al mismo tiempo acallar otros hechos de Don José Antonio Navarro, cuya apuntacion no nos perdonaria su delicada modestia apesar del consentimiento que nos dá en su carta—contestacion, y que está al principio de este cuaderno.

Baste lo dicho ya, para que todos los que conocen al H. Don José Antonio Navarro, vean que hemos escrito en obsequio de la verdad, cuyo medio esperamos que sirva de manifiesto para todos aquellos que como nosotros, le profesen un verdadero afecto.

San Antonio Junio 20 de 1869.

N. Leal y varios amigos.

Apuntes historicos interesantes.

Sr. Editor del Ledger:

Como en los números 27 y 28 del mes de Diciembre de 1853 de éste periódico que vmd. ahora redacta, publicó el autor de estos apuntes los sucesos acaecidos en los años de 1812 y 1813 de la invacion del General Bernardo Gutierres, que fue quien por primera vez trajo de los Estados-Unidos aquellos seiscientos ó mas voluntarios è intrépidos Norte-Americanos auxiliares de la Independencia Mexicana; que despues de haberse batido por cerca de diez meses contra las tropas del Rey de España en frente de las murallas de Goliad y en los campos del Rosillo, y Alazan; al fin sucumbieron en la sangrienta batalla de Medina el 18 de Agosto del año de 1813 contra una fuerza numérica que el veterano General Español Joaquin de Arredondo traia del interior de México; parece que no será de menos interes para los lectores, especialmente para los actuales habitantes de Goliad y de San Antonio y al rededores, donde sus deliciosas florestas y sus cristalinos manantiales están salpicados con las gotas de sangre ilustre que desde tantos años atras vertieron muchos defensores de la libertad; leer y saber ahora por la boca de un co temporaneo, testigo ocular, el origen y como comenzaron tantos hechos romanticos, en que tomaron una parte activa los heroicos hijos naturales de la ciudad de San Antonio de Bexar desde el año de 1811 para adelante.

Ageno de toda pretencion literaria, fanatico habitual, en materia historica, contra toda produccion mercenaria, escribo este opúsculo sintiendome libre y superior á los que lo hagan por especulacion; los hechos que narro se fixaron desde su tiempo, en mi retina y no tengo necesidad de buscar perifrasis ni alegorias como para los cuentos mitologicos.

Papel, tinta y plumas con un ardiente deseo de que algun habil, y veridico historiador futuro tenga materiales con que engalanar la historia de este mi amado pais, he aqui lo que me ha hecho escribir y en lo que se cifra un ambicion moral y recompensa pecuniaria.

El público habrá visto la historia de Texas escrita por el malogrado coronel Yoakum; que aunque en muchos respectos apreciable y exacta, está plagada de algunas inexactitudes como por exemplo, la de hacer morir degollado en el Rosillo al Gobernador Antonio Cordero entre los catorce oficiales Españoles que fueron alli asesinados; cuando es constante que Cordero vivia aun, hasta el año de 1821 en México: dice igualmente que el padre del capitan Antonio Delgado fué fucilado en San Antonio y puesta su cabeza á la espectacion pública y cuando sabemos bien, que aquel venerable viejo murió de vejez y pesadumbre en el rio de Trinidad, cuando Elizondo iba persiguiendo á los prófugos de la batalla de Medina: por este tenor incide el coronel Yoakum en otros pequeños errores, que aunque no injurian á lo sustancial de la historia; importan una peripecia inconciliable, como cuando dice, *que por causa de la guerra de los indios las tropas del Alamo estuvieron compelidos* allá por el año de 1785 á repelgarse dentro de las murallas de la Mision, eso és cierto que sucedió; pero fué cuando esas tropas estaban en el llamado Alamo de Parras en México y mucho antes de que hubieran venido á este Alamo de la Mision de San Antonio Valero; la cual se llamó asi desde su fundacion y solamente tuvo el sobre nombre de Alamo, despues que las tropas del Alamo de Parras vinieron á la Mision de Valero que fue allá por los años de 1803 á 1804 y subsistieron en esta Mision sin mudanza ninguna hasta la revolucion de 1843.

Estos motivos y las instancias de algunos de mis amigos que han deseado saber los mas importantes sucesos contemporaneos acaecidos en nuestra ciudad, me han decidido á escribir esta sucinta crónica.

No la hago para las almas pequeñas, ni para los egoistas, que poco ó nada les importan las glorias ó desgracias de hombres de otro origen y lenguaje: la hago para los filántropos y cosmopolitas, que saben apreciar y condolerse de las vicisitudes de un pueblo valiente, que ha luchado enmedio de su propia ignorancia y por solo el instinto de su libertad, con enemigos tan superio-

6

res; por tal de ponerse al nivel de los hombres mas libres y dichosos del género humano, como son los que cubre el pabellon de las estrellas: la hago para que sepa nuestro pueblo Americano, cuan indignamente hay algunos entre nosotros, que con pretextos mesquinos ó ingratos quieren extirpar de este suelo clásico, á los legítimos señores y descendientes de los que hace como medio siglo que derramaron su sangre, buscando esa libertad de que hacemos jactancia.

Desde los años de 1807 y 1808 que la nacion española parecia estar dando las últimas boqueadas por la invación de aquel prodigio de conquistadores, Napoleon 1 °, los Mexicanos comenzaron sus conferencias privadas, á fin de sacudir el yugo ominoso de la madre patria; no porque le vieran despedazada y casi absorvida por el formidable conquistador, sino porque no podian ya tolerar el enxambre de tiranuelos Españoles, que en su rabiosa inpotencia, en su frenetico delírio que les causaban los quebrantos de la Peninsula Española, venian á descargar sobre los mansos hijos de México crueldades no imagenables, acompañados de exacciones pequniarias que les arrancaban con violencia, para repartirse este valioso botin entre las tumultuosas Juntas y Gobiernos, llamados provinciales de España.

Jamás pueblo alguno de la tierra y mosaico mas confusamente taraceado, de órden y disposiciones, todas dirijuas á la oprecion y la rapiña contra el desgraciado pueblo Mexicano.

El dia 8 de Setiembre de 1808 un General Frances llamado Octabiano D'Alvimar llegó á San Antonio de Bexar: se dijo que habia atravesado de incógnito los Estados-Unidos y entró á Texas por Nacogdoches, era D'Alvimar, precisamente, el preconizado virrey de México, que mandaba Napoleon.

Le vimos entrar en la plaza de San Antonio con su vistoso uniforme, cubierto de placas y de cruces brillantes, que contrastab n con el benigno sol que todavia alumbraba la plaza de San Antonio, antes de llegar á su ocaso; pero el General D'Alvimar parece que aun ignoraba todavia los reveces de fortuna de su amo el Emperador y que el sobervio é indómito pueblo Español estaba ya corriendo en arroyos de sangre, para sacudir la dominacion Francesa en España. Ignoraba, que òrdenes astutas é Inquisitoriales, peculiares de la diplomácia Española en transiciones emergentes, estaban ya anticipadas por el Virreynato, á fin que D'Alvimar fuese hecho prisionero y remitido con seguridad á la capital México, como lo fué, por dispocicion del Gobernador de la Provincia, Don Antonio Cordero.

Parece que este incidente anunciaba algunos triunfos de los Españoles en la Península y mas terror para las tentativas de los conspiradores en América; pero no obstante, los Mexicanos siguieron sus conspiraciones secretas para independerse de la Metropolí.

Por otra parte las noticias que llegaban de la peninsula cada dia, eran tristes y alarmantes: las tropas de Napoleon triunfaban por todas partes y los Españoles empezaban por millaradas á jurar obediencia al Emperador de los Franceses.

Se supo por fin, que un magistrado Frances vendria en breve, mandado por Napoleon á recibir y encargarse del Vireynato de México.

El cura del pueblo de Dolores, Don Miguel Hidalgo era uno de los conspiradores: el grito de Independencia estaba preparado para cierto dia, mas un Arnold Mexicano que estaba en el secreto, dió aviso anticipado al virrey de México y acaso menos de dos horas despues de las 12 de la noche del 16 de Setiembre de 1810 en que dió el grito el cura Hidalgo, hubieran bastado para haberlo hecho prisionero, mandado á México y concluido con toda esperanza de independencia.

¡Viva Nuestra Señora de Guadalupe y mueran los Gachupines! fué la primera invocacion que le ocurrió en momentos tan perentorios: bajo de auspicios tan debiles fué nacida una revolucion fecunda en resultados, que ha criado una República federativa que figura entre la familia de las Naciones.

El que quiera juzgar con asombro esas anomalias, detengase primero á contemplar las épocas y las capacidades del pueblo donde sucedieron: coloquese en el lugar del patriota Hidalgo: denunciado ya como traidor, ante el inplacable déspota Virrey de México: conciderese en una situacion apremiable; sin plan de operaciones de ninguna especie, sin dinero ni armas, ni tropa: sin mas que unos sentenares de Indios de su propio pueblo: masas informes y estupidas, á quienes ni el severo raciocinio de un Washington, ni la voluntad fuerte de un Napoleon 1°, podrian haber conducido á empresa tan Magna, sino era moviendolas por la venganza y supersticion, como estubo compelido á hacerle, este Ilustre y desventurado Patriota.

Por una consecuencia necesaria, se siguió desde allí el pillaje y el degüello; ¡pero poderosos son los instintos del pueblo que pelea por una justa causa! Los Mexicanos, en medio de aquellos desordenes inevitables, triunfaban por todas partes hasta fines de 1810.

Por todos los confines del reino se habian levantado en masa, expeliendo, aprisionando ó degollando á los Españoles, los ecos de los triunfos insurgentes, se oyeron por todas las mas remotas provincias, y este dia llegó para San Antonio de Bexar.

Una guarnicion de 2,000 soldados del Rey cubria esta ciudad y los puntos militares, hasta el rio de Sabinas: sus principales ordenes eran las de resguardar la provincia de Texas á todo azar, contra las tentativas de los EstadosUnidos, estaban aquí la oficialidad y tropa mas lucidas de Nuevo-Leon y Nuevo-Santander: cada soldado se puede decir que, era un ciudadano capitalista: un distinguido á quien el Virrey de México asistia con predileccion. ¿Que es de extrañarse, que en ese tiempo, San Antonio estubiera en el apogeo de su prosperidad? Centenares de miles de oro y plata acuñadas ingresaban á la ciudad cada dos meses, para la esmerada mantencion de las tropas. Cosa muy comun era, ver á un soldado cualquiera, expender cien pesos en una merienda y con la misma serenidad que convidariamos ahora á un amigo, para tomar un vaso de serveza.

Con todo y estos plaseres individuales que se disfrutaban, como la vida de un gran pueblo pertenece á toda la sociedad humana, los ciudadanos y tropas de San Antonio empezaban á manifestar alguna anciedad por la suerte política de México: hablillas y acriminaciones se hacian ya notar en las conversaciones amistosas, en contra de los Gobernantes Españoles.

Los descendientes de los primeros Isleños, pobladores de Bexar como legitimos señores originales, eran los que con mas libre osadia descubrian los conatos de humillar la altaneria de los Gobernadores Españoles, Delgados, Arochas, Leales, Traviesos y otros que formaban en Bexar unas tribus privilegiadas, se consideraban los nobles desde que sus Padres vinieron de las Islas canarias á poblar la Provincia de Texas el año de 1730.

De aquí dimanaban su bien pretendido orgullo y la celoza indignacion contra las acciones despoticas de los Gobernadores Españoles. No podia haber coyuntura mas adecuada para estos resentidos nobles, que la que ofrecian las noticias de México, con respecto á los triunfos alcanzados por el cura Hidalgo y los demas Gefes insurreccionados.

Habia sin embargo, un considerable obstaculo para efectuarse el pronunciamiento: los principales Gefes Militares eran de origen Español: habia algunos otros de origen Mexicano pero estos se detenian por respetuosa delicadeza á iniciarse los primeros, contra los derechos del monarca que habia dominado por 300 años.

En este conflicto de intereses opuestos, los ciudadanos escogieron individuos del Exército; que ni fueran oficiales de alta graduacior, á quienes la delicadeza del empleo los inutilizara para la empresa, ni fueran simples soldados; á quien la couciencia de su inferioridad les compeliera á retroceder en la hora del peligro.

Tres sargentos pues, fueron los escogidos para seducir el Exército, y fueron Miguel Reyna, Blas José Perales y Trinidad Perez: estos pusieron toda la tropa sobre las armas e. los cuarteles que estaban donde ahora llaman la Villita, al Este de San Antonio.

Al amanecer del dia 22 de Enero de 1811 ofrecieron este Exército al capitan de milicias del Nuevo-Sautander, Juan Bautista Casas, quien admitió el mando ofrecido y se puso á la cabeza de mil quinientos hombres.

Casas marchó en columnas para la plaza de Gobierno, le acompañaban como representando á los ciudadanos, Don Gavino Delgado, Don Francisco Travieso y Don Vicente Flores: muy apenas empesaria el alboréo del dia, cuando ya los Batallones estaban en columna cerrada, frente á la plaza de Gobierno.

El capitan Casas con su Estado Mayor entró é hizo prisioneros á los Gobernadores Salcedo, Herrera y otros mas oficiales Españoles, que aun dormian todavia el plácido sueño de los crépusculos de la mañana, confiados, de que ninguno atentaria contra sus personas omnipotentes.

Este dia memorable del 22 de Enero de 1811 fué el primero en que los Mexicanos de San Antonio de Bejar anunciaron querer romper para siempre las cadenas de su envejecida esclavitud colonial.

Este fué el dia en que esforzandose para disimular aquella voz temblona y gutural que infunde la larga vida servil, pudieron hablarles alto, á los que antes habian sido los amos absolutos de los Mexicanos.

Pero esa mutacion repentina de hoy, en que los esclavos se elevaron á señores y árbitros de sus opresores y amos de ayer, crió la vanguardia mas amarga contra los llamados gachupines.

El capitan Casas se apresuró á remitir catorce gefes Españoles, bien cargados de cadenas, para el interior de México.

El 16 de Febrero del mismo año salieron de Bexar con una formidable guardia, al mando de los mismos Don Vicente Flores y sargento Miguel Reyna, con órdenes de entregar los presos al Brigadier insurgente Don Pedro Aranda, que se hallaban en el Presidio del Rio Grande.

Todo parecia indicar el triunfo, seguro de la Independencia mexicana y apenas habria alguno que no envidiara la gloria de los que se habian atrevido á encadenar á los opresores Españoles.

Pero como es hoy de la naturaleza humana, que mientras mas vehementes son los accesos del ánimo, mas instantánea sea su duracion, muy pocos dias transcurrieron sin observarse semblantes melancólicos que aun mal disimulados, como el enfermo que afecta desconocer lo grave de su enfermedad para no admitir el eproximado fin de su excistencia; no se podia dejar señas mas trágicas que las del 22 de Enero.

Casas y los demas corífeos, fingiendo desconocer todo peligro, dexaban libremente que las masas del pueblo y la tropa de la guarnicion hicieran comentarios sobre las noticias que llegaban de México, en que se ecsageraban las derrotas sufridas por el cura Hidalgo y se pintaba la situacion desesperada de los Ejércitos Independientes.

¡Era ello, desgraciadamente la verdad! las glorias de Hidalgo, Allende, Abasolo y otros ilustres capitanes de la Independencia, se habian eclipsado en las inmediaciones de la capital de México y ya hacian por retirarse con su derrotado Ejército para las Provincias de Coahuila y de Texas, con mas de cinco millones en oro y plata acuñada; con fin de internarse para los Estados-Unidos y proporcionarse un grande Ejército de voluntarios Americanos.

¡Inescrutables juicios de la alta providencia! ¿Que hombre mortal se atreverá á investigar sus divinas disposiciones? pero permítenos como desahogos de nuestro filial sentimiento, preguntar, ¿porqué no permitiste que esos infortunados héroes posasen con esos valiosos caudales á la tierra clásica de los Estados-Unidos del Norte; evitando así esos diez años de guerra cruel, en que desaparecieron mas de quinientos mil Mexicanos, muertos en los campos y en los patíbulos?........ pero echamos un velo respetuoso sobre los arcanos, donde no debe penetrar la razon humana y sigamos los sucesos que pasaban en San Antonio de Bexar.

El capitan Juan Bautista Casas, era natural de San Fernando en la antigua Provincia de Nuevo-Santander: pertenecia á la compañia de Milicias de Croix y era cuando murió, de edad de 36 años: aunque era capitalista en su pais, servia el empleo militar por honor: sus talentos eran medianos; pero desinteresado y honrado: admitió el mando que le ofrecieron los ciudadanos y la guarnicion Militar de San Antonio, porque creyó que era llegado el tiempo de combatir contra los enemigos naturales de su pátria, y mas que todo; porque era hombre de aquellos que por una exciva urbanidad son incapaces de negarse á la suplica y la importunidad.

Este es el hombre que se puso á la cabeza de aquel volcan revolucionario: el que se halló entre un pueblo sin estrategia guerrera, sin principios políticos y sin mas guia que el ciego inpulso de la venganza: elementos discordientes, que facilitaron á los Españoles la introduccion de sus emisarios y proclamas, con que facilmente dispusieron los ánimos, para lo que se llamó á la contrarevolucion ó sea volver de nuevo á la obediencia del tirano Rey de España.

El Padre Juan Manuel Zambrano, hijo de Bexar, de cuerpo agigentado y obeso de arrogante presencia; tan vivo y volátil como el azogue y de una inclinacion especial para toda azonada, fué designado para efectuar la contrarevolucion en favor de los Españoles.

No es mi ánimo increpar la conducta de los que tomaron parte en esta contrarevolucion que apresuró el patíbulo del infortunado Casas; sino mas bien deplorar y compadecer el extravio de la razon de los que, imbuidos con el falso honor de ser fieles al tirano mas detestable de Europa, hicieron á alarde de enterrar el puñal fratricida en el corazon de sus hermanos Mexicanos: de remachar así sus propias cadenas y de seguir derramando lágrimas para ganar el pan cüotidiano, tras del paso tardio de los agenos Bueyes.

El dia 3 de Marzo del mismo año de 1811 fué sorprendido y hecho prisionero Juan Bautista Casas por el dicho Padre, Juan Manuel Zambrano, en las mismas casas de Gobierno donde 39 dias antes se habian aprisionado á los Gobernadores y con las mismas tropas.

Se rindió Casas con la serenidad de un valiente; mas al verse rodeado de bayonetas de aquellos mismos que hacia pocos dias habian sido sus amigos y complices; como les dijo con indignacion, ¿sois vosotros, los mismos que me colocasteis en este puesto y ahora venceis á añadir la infama á la traicion, cautivandome para entregarme á un patíbulo?

Callad, miserable traidor, le contestó uno de los aprehensores, con aquella fanática y verbosa conviccion, como cuando los inquisidores iban á quemar con leña verde y bajo el santo nombre de Dios á los llamados hereges, ¡callad! y someteos á la Justicia, ó la clemencia de nuestro muy amado soberano, en el señor Don Fernando Septimo.

¡Que viva el Rey! y á esta voz de trueno, un repique general de las campanas, los vivas de la tropa y del Pueblo, con una algarabia farisáica, semejante la que forman los salvages antropófagos alrededor de la victima que van á sacrificar, quedó anunciado que el desdichado capitan Casas estaba entre cadenas y los habitantes de San Antonio volvian otra vez á la clase de vasallos del Rey de España.

Dejemos al pobre Casas gimiendo entre sus cadenas dentro de un calaboso inmundo y solitario, para ver lo que por ese mismo tiempo estaba ocurriendo del otro lado del Rio Grande.

Ya hemos dicho que desde el 16 de Febrero habian sido remitidos en prision los Gobernadores Salcedo, Herrera y los demas oficiales, haciendo un total de catorce presos. Estos habian ya llegado á Monclova: El Coronel Mexicano Ignacio Elizondo se hallaba allí, pronunciado en favor del Rey: estaban puestos en libertad Salcedo, Herrera y oficiales: todos unidos forxaban el modo mas seguro de atraer con ingenio al cura Hidalgo con su Ejército que ya estaba en la villa del Saltillo, para por medio de una estratagema hacerlo prisionero: cuando esto sucedia, debe saberse que ya todas las provincias del Norte de México empezaron á pronunciarse por la causa del Rey.

El presidente Zambrano traslucia ya todo esto en Bexar: mas sin embargo, con aquella superchería que tenian por virtud estratégica los revolucionarios de ese tiempo, envió prontamente Zambrano dos emisarios de su confianza, que fueron los capitanes José Muños y Luis Galan: salieron el 8 de Marzo con instrucciones dobles y adecuadas, para manejarse en aquella embajada, en caso de encontrarse con el Cura Hidalgo ó con los Generales del Rey; pues el caso era quedarse bien parados con uno y otro de los partidos beligerantes.

Causa compasion, mas bien que horror, contemplar las tortuosidades rastreras á que la Maquiavélica enseñanza de los altos gefes Españoles, habia conducido á los incautos Mexicanos, patrocinando entre ellos los hechos mas indignos de veleidad y de traicion, con la inicua mira de apagar en sus pechos todo sentimiento generoso y constituirlos viles instrumentos de su propia destruccion.

Muñós y Galan al llegar á Monclova, viendo que ya todo estaba dispuesto en favor del Rey, ofrecieron, á los Gobernadores Españoles la grata noticia de quedar aprisionado en Bexar el traidor Casas y por consiguiente las congratulaciones de los fieles vasallos de su Magestad en todo Texas.

Pusieron inmediatamente un correo expreso para comunicar al Presidente Zambrano el feliz resultado de su diplomatica mision, suplicandole al mismo tiempo que remitiese lo mas pronto posible para Monclova al prisionero Casas, donde se le esperaba para purgar ofensas hechas al soberano; pero Zambrano era ya un maestro mas consumado, en la ciencia de los ardides, que sus preceptores los Españoles: detuvo la remision de Casas hasta mejor asegurarse del estado que guardaban las cosas del interior de México.

Con noticias bien ciertas de la bien organizada conspiracion de Monclova, en que infaliblemente seria hecho prisionero todo el ejército del cura Hidalgo, remitió al ilustre cautivo el dia 2 de Julio del mismo año de 1811 bajo una guardia mandada por el sargento de la Bahia Juan José Calderon.

Zambrano salió tambien el dia 26 del mismo mes, acompañado de su junta Gobernativa y todas las tropas de San Antonio, á un paseo Militar hasta la Villa de Laredo.

Casas arribó á Monclova como á mediados del mes de Julio: Cordero y los demas Gobernadores Españoles estaban allí, era el foco Monclova, de todos los próceres castellanos, como que se esperaban las visperas Sicilianas contra el desgraciado Hidalgo.

A Casas se le siguió su causa criminal que fué vista en consejo de guerra Militar, de quien el mismo Cordero fué el presidente: Salió condenado unanimemente á ser pasado por las armas.

Cuando se le vino á leer su sentencia· de muerte, por el Fiscal, Casas se puso de rodillas, la oyó y despues besó aquel papel de la fatal admocion, segun es la costumbre.

¡Pobre de Casas! era un cristiano ortodoxo y sincero: cuando se le preguntó si algo tenia que decir sobre su sentencia, respondió: „No! porque conosco que he faltado à mi soberano: solamente quisiera alcanzar una gracia de su real clemencia y es: que una corta cantidad del producto de mis bienes, se reservase para darsela á mi anciana y pobre madre, para la mantencion de sus últimos dias: los reales tesoros de su Magostad son grandes y ninguna falta le hará la pequeñes de lo que se separe de mis bienes: tambien deseo suplicar, que se paguen cosa de dosientos pesos que estoy debiendo y no tengo arbitrio de pagarlos, si se confiscan todos mis intereses despues de mi muerte: no tengo mas que pedir."

Como ya se sabia que estaba para llegar á Acatita de Bajan, el Exército del cura Hidalgo, se suspendió la execucion de Casas.

El dia 27 de Julio fué hecho prisionero el cura Hidalgo, con treinta y dos generales y todo el Estado mayor, dòs mil y mas hombres de tropa y poco mas de tres y medio millones de oro y plata acuñado: todo cayò en manos de Elizondo y los Gobernadores.

Hidalgo y los mas de los generales fueron conducidos hasta Chihuahua y fusilados. Despues de este acontecimiento, es decir, el dia 1º de Agosto, se puso en capilla á Casas y se le pasó por las armas en Monclova el dia 3 del mismo mes, al pie de la loma que llaman de Zapopa: Se mandó cortarle la cabeza, que fué remitida á San Antonio de Bexar: aunque llegó en tres dias y medio ya estaba pútrida y se mandó enterrar.

El General Bernardo Gutierres, coronel entonces del Exército de Hidalgo, sabiendo lo acaecido el 27 de Julio, se salió fugitivo y pasando por los desiertos de Texas, arribó á los Estados-Unidos, desde donde trajo los voluntarios Americanos para la campaña de 1812 y 1813.

Hemos visto ya la efímera duracion de la Independencia Mexicana en Texas el año de 1811, el fin tragico de Casas y lo apagado que quedaron todas las esperanzas de libertad: los Gobernadores Españoles volvieron de Monclova para asumir sus antiguos puestos en el mando.

El Presidente Zambrano y junta Gobernativa entregaron el mando á los oficiales del Rey. El pueblo de San Antonio volvió á sus atributos exlusivos: obedecer ciegamente á un Rey del cielo, á otro de la tierra y trabajar para ganar el pan.

Al pensar en esta dulce conformidad de un sencillo Pueblo, fijando toda su ambicion y felicidad temporal y eterna, en agradar á un soberano celestial y á otro terrestre; naturalmente ocurre la cuestion, de, si seria mas conforme con la dicha del genero humano, reducir todos sus pensamientos y obligaciones al obedecimiento de solamente dos agentes superiores, (áun dado caso de pensar que eran inaptos) antes que meterse el hombre á esas amargas y dificiles molestias, de querer examinar, comprender y manejar, todos los eslabones de la intrincada maquina de un gobierno? ¡Si seria mas acomodado para la salud del cuerpo y la tranquilidad del espiritu, vivir en ignorancia supina, de los poderes de los hombres y de los Gobernantes, para no tener el sentimiento de ver p conocer el Exército de malvados del Mundo; que prevalidos de la fueza brutal unos y con el ropage de libertad é igualdad otros, roban y asesinan á los indigentes y en muchas circunstancias vilipendian á ~~los indigentes mismos~~ los mismos que les han dado patria y poder?

Pero semejante dulce paz que gozaban á favor de esa ciega obediencia pasiva, si de descarse fuera, ya entraba en los alborotados corazones de los nobles Isleños: nuevas aspiraciones se habian transmitido desde la República vecina del Norte, al travez de los mares y por entre las estrechas veredas de los, entonces desiertos de Texas.

El gusto por las ideas y costumbres ultramontanas se marchitaba ante las incomparables satisfacciones de un Pueblo-rey, de la america, los raquiticos gobernantes Españoles, debian desmoronarse muy en breve, contra la fuerza moral de instituciones republicanas.

Tales ideas abrigaban estos nobles Isleños y las descubrieron mas tarde; aunque sin mas ventura, que envolverse en ruinas y quedar casi extingidos del suelo que les vió nacer y habian conquistado sus Padres.

Apenas 16 meses llegaban desde la catástrofe de Acatota de Bajan, cuando Bernardo Gutierrez entró á Texas, por Noviembre de 1812 con aquel corto Exército de Leonidas Norte-Americanos y tomó la Bahia y seguidamente San Antonio, en 1 ° del mes de Abril de 1812.

Inmediatamente los Delgados, Arochas, Traviesos, Leales y otros muchos acordandose de lo que habian sufrido el año anterior por la causa de Independencia, se unieron á Gutierrez y su banda, en cuerpo y amor.

Conbatieron con ardor y entusiasmo contra el poder del terrible Arredondo: triunfó este en la célebre batalla de Medina y estos patriotas quedaron muertos en los campos y en los patíbulos: muy pocos emigraron para los Estados-Unidos, para no volver jamás: todo lo perdiercn estos valerosos espiritus.

La Independencia Mexicana, germinada con la sangre de estos mártires, se declaró por fin en México en Setiembre de 1821.

Pero ¡oh dolor!.... un solo suspiro atravezó jamas las montañas de Anahuac, para venir á consolar siquiera á los desolados restos de aquellos Patriotas esforzados.

¡Asi fenecer los héroes! tal vez sea mas completa en gloria, que si recibieran las mozquinas conpesaciones de los hombres.

Para completar el cuadro de infortunios, los pocos vástagos que aun sobre viven en San Antonio están desapareciendo asesinados, á la vista de un pueblo que blazona de justo y grande por exelencia.

Doña Consolacion Leal, heroína de aquel tiempo, hace pocos meses que murió asesinada por un Español y Don Antonio Delgado, fué atravezado por las balas del rifle de un bastardo Americano.

Quiera el cielo que la lectura de estos trozos historicos, hagan palpitar á los corazones generosos, para tratar con mas indulgencia á esa raza de hombres, que dueños legitimos de este pais, lo perdieron, juntamente con sus vidas y sus esperanzas, por seguir las huellas de esos mismos, que hoy le gozan en medio de la paz y de la abundancia.— J. A. N.

Bajo este rubro comenzamos á publicar en el número 11 de nuestro Boletin, los que escribió el Sr. J. A. N. de San Antonio de Bexar y en nuestro número de hoy concluye dicha publicacion.

La descripcion está llena de interes porque su autor como testigo contemporáneo y como partícipe en los mas importantes acontecimientos de la época á que se contrae, poseido ademas, de un sentimiento de gratitud y filantrópia hacia su pais natal, y adornado de una despejada capacidad y despreocupada inteligencia, ha presentado las cosas y los hombres tal como fueron, como se le fijaron desde aquel tiempo sin ambajes ni alegorias y sin mas pretencion ni otra ambicion que la verdad historica aproveche de sus apuntes. Exitamos por lo mismo, al D. J. A. N. á que continúe sus importantes trabajos no solo de la época conocida por la Insurreccion, sino hasta la del fatal cambio político que produjó la Independencia, memorable campaña y pérdida de Texas por parte de México acontecimientos de que ha

sido teatro principal la ciudad de San Antonio por su posicion y sus elementos respectivamente de las demas poblaciones Texanas, dandole la enhora-
buena por lo bien recibidas que han sido hasta ahora sus importantes tareas
históricas. *)

Apuntes historicos de San Antonio de Bexar.
Por un testigo ocular.

„Los siguientes recuerdos históricos que fueron escritos en español para el
Ledger, fueron puestos en planta la semana pasada, pero se suspendieron
por una súplica del Caballero que ayudó en la traduccion diciendo que el
manuscrito necesitaba algun adereso por lo que no pudo salir á tiempo
en nuestro número de la semana pasada; de entonces acá ha resuelto que
el citado opúsculo estaba „demasiado bueno" para darsele publicidad en los
periódicos de San Antonio, y sabemos que lo ha mandado publicar á otra
parte sin consultar á su autor, esto ocasionó la dilacion de nuestro número
en la semana anterior, y nos ha puesto en la necesidad de procurar otra traduccion privandonos así de dar á luz el articulo entero en esta semana."

Al Editor del Ledger de San Antonio;

Respetable Señor:— En su número del 17 de Setiembre prócsimo pasado
leí unos recuerdos históricos de la fundacion é historia antigua de San Antonio de Bexar: como yo fui un testigo ocular de todas las ocurrencias que se
destacan en ella, no puedo resistir á la tentacion de corregir algunos errores
sustanciales, contenidos en esa narracion. Indudablemente resultan de informes inexactos, quizá sacados de documentos truncos y mutilados en los
que es difícil seguir la cadena histórica. Siempre se ha deseado obtener el
mas fiel informe de esos sucesos, pues presentan á la posteridad las costumbres, carácter, capacidad y cualidades morales de los hombres y las cosas de
aquella época.—En 1813 el autor de esta comunicacion rayaba en los 18 años
de edad —Estaba entonces en San Antonio y aun retiene frescos los recuerdos de aquel periodo.—Esta circunstancia y el deseo de que cuanto conoier-
na á San Antonio, querido por mil razones, producen la presente efusion, y
deberian ser relatadas con el respeto mas debido á la verdad.—No descubri-
reis en ella floreos ni empeño en la excelencia de su estilo sino una narracion sin ambajes de tiempos revolucionarios y sangrientos. Un Cura mexicano llamadose Miguel Hidalgo y Costilla ilustre por mil títulos, fué real-
mente el primero en dar el grito de independencia en el pueblo de Dolores.
El cura Don José Maria Morelos célebre de entonces á acá por sus talentos
militares, fué tambien otro de los héroes de la Independencia Mexicana y
quien luego despúes de la ejecucion del cura Hidalgo convocó el primer con-
greso mexicano llamado de Apacingán. El General Don Félix Maria Calleja, despues virey de México se distinguió con particularidad por las perse-
cuciones sanguinarias é inicuas contra los patriotas, Hidalgo, Guerrero, Morelos, Bravo y otros.—Calleja fué el mas formidable enemigo de los mexicanos.

Morelos fué capturado, tratado con ignominia y finalmente fusilado en el
Castillo viejo de San Cristoval á cuatro leguas distante de la Capital de

*) Las Apuntes escritos al principio de este cuaderno son una parte publicada en
el „Boletin del Pueblo" periódico publicado en Camargo en 1858, de donde los tomamos juntamente con el párrafo que le precede.

14

México. Don José Bernardo Gutierrez nativo de Revilla de Tamaulipas salió para los Estados-Unidos inmediatamente despues de la aprehencion y prision de los patriotas héroes en Acatita de Bajan cerca de Monclova en el año de 1811.

Visitó á Washington y otros puntos de los Estados-Unidos, y por fin convocó en el Estado de Luisiana cosa de cuatrocientos cincuenta voluntarios americanos con los que invadió de nuevo á Texas en el mes de Octubre de 1812. Nacogdoches fortificacion militar sobre el rio de la Trinidad fué tomada por él, sin resistencia, y subsecuentemente lo fué la Bahia del Espiritu Santo, hoy Goliad. Don Manuel Salcedo, Gobernador Militar de Texas, y Don Simon de Herrera, de Nuevo Leon, salieron con mas de dos mil hombres y pusieron sitio á la Bahia el 15 de Noviembre del mismo año.

Los Generales Gutierres, Mc. Gee, Kemper, Perry y Ross sostuvieron el sitio por el período amargo de tres meses. Desesperados al fin los sitiados salieron fuera de las murallas de Goliad con casi toda la fuerza compuesta de voluntarios americanos y algunos mexicanos, se batieron con el enemigo, y por fin volvieron á entrar al fuerte, dejando 200 del enemigo muertos y heridos, y sufriendo ellos menos pérdida. Despues de veinte y siete encuentros regulares, Salcedo y Herrera levantaron el sitio y se retiraron á San Antonio á fines de Marzo de 1813. Gutierres, Kemper y otros, animados por la retirada violenta del enemigo lo siguieron dia á dia. No habia llegado Salcedo á San Antonio con su ejército, cuando se le ordenó por Don Simon de Herrera que abandonase la Ciudad y marchase al Salado, á donde en el paraje llamadose el „Rosillo" encuentró al ejército de Gutierres, si á una banda de 900 patriotas pudiera llamársele tal. Las dos fuerzas marchaban juntas á fines de Marzo. La batalla fué sangrienta. Herrera perdió 400 hombres entre muertos y heridos, y Gutierres no tuvo mas que 5 muertos y 14 heridos. El ejército realista corrió en desórden con rumbo á San Antonio, que Salcedo y Herrera habian comenzado á fortificar con intencion de resistir á Gutierres.

Este Kemper y otros, despues de recojer los despojos de la batalla y enterrar sus muertos, los persiguieron con su ejército victorioso y se posecionaron de la Mision de la Concepcion al Sudeste de San Antonio. Al siguiente dia marcharon para Bexar. El ejército de patriotas formado en columnas dobles en la labor llamada de abajo á donde las residencias particulares de los SS. Divine, Callaghan y Gilban están ahora: desde ese memorable precinto. Don Bernardo Gutierres, intimó la rendicion incondicional de los Gobernadores Salcedo y Herrera. Este tuvo lugar el 30 de Marzo de 1813. En el 31 por la tarde estos mismos personages con su Estado Mayor y otros gefes de alta graduacion, salieron de Bexar á pié al encuentro de Gutierres y su ejército victorioso. Fué muy corta la conferencia entre los victoriosos y vencidos, nada se sabe de lo que pasó, escepto la garantia de sus vidas que pidieron los vencidos. Gutierres contestandoles con evasivas les dió á entender que no habia peligro en sus vidas.

Aquellos infortunados gefes españoles se rindieron á discresion y así por su cobardia sellaron su suerte. Entregaron sus espadas y fueron puestos entre dos filas. Gutierres y su ejército volvieron á pasar al lado oriental del rio, haciendo marchar al frente sus prisioneros al son de una música marcial y entraron en las murallas del Alamo. El mismo „Alamo que en Marzo de 836 habia de ser la cuna de la libertad de Texas ó escenas de prodigios de valor. Alli los valientes patriotas Gutierres, Kemper, Ross y sus bravos compañeros reposaron el primer sueño del triunfo en la noche del 31 de Marzo. Alli sellaron ellos el misterioso legado de esos terribles sucesos ocurridos en el año de 1836.

El 1 º de Abril á las 9 de la mañana marchó el ejército republicano á tambor batiente de el Alamo á la plaza principal de San Antonio. Pasaron el rio sobre un puente miserable, sustituido hoy con otro hermoso y exelente sobre la calle del comercio. El ejército hispano–mexicano se habian desbandado y retirado en la noche anterior, y no se veia en ninguna parte de la Ciudad. Solo algunas personas sobrecogidas del terror, y las familias de algunos ciudadanos de San Antonio permanecieron. Gutierrez tomó posesion de las casas de Gobierno, á donde la hermosa tienda de los señores Vances está ahora, é inmediatamente convocó una junta administrativa ó consejo civil de aquellos nativos que con mas ardor se oponian al mando español y que consiguientemente favorecian la independencia mexicana: esta junta la componian de ocho á diez miembros, un presidente y un secretario. Por lo que ha escrito Gutierrez parece que la hizo firmar con el solo objeto de enjuiciar y sentenciar militarmente á los prisioneros españoles. El secretario de esta junta Don Mariano Rodrigues vive aun, era entonces un jóven vivo y alegre, hoy es anticuado septuagenario que vejeta en San Antonio con muy limitado recuerdo del pasado y estremo descuido del futuro. El dia 2 de Abril ó tal vez en la noche del 5 una partida de 60 hombres, todos mexicanos bajo el mando del capitan Don Antonio Delgado, sacó de San Antonio los 14 prisioneros españoles inclusos 4 de orijen mexicano, al lado oriental del Salado, cerca del mismo lugar en donde se dió la batalla del Rosillo adonde se apearon de sus caballos primorosos, y sin otras armas que los velduques botos que cada uno de esos mónstruos cargaba pendiente del cinto, para uso del campo, los degollaron despues de haberles colmado de injuriosos palabras y epitetos insultantes. Algunos de esos asesinos, con ironia inhumana afilaron sus velduques en la suela de sus zapatos á presencia de sus víctimas indefensas.

¡Oh Vergüenza del genero humano.! ¡Oh, desgracia de los descendientes de una nacion cristiana!

Que sangre puede con frialdad sufrir en silencio un acto sin ejemplo en los anales de la historia de San Antonio de Bexar? Pero debemos una historia imparcial á la posteridad que haga conocer tan enormes hechos á las generaciones venideras, para que con su buena conducta futura puedan erradicar manchas tan horrendas de nuestro benigno suelo. Un dia despues de la matanza, yo mismo vi llegar á esa horda de asesinos, con su gefe Antonio Delgado, quien hizo alto al frente de las casas de Gobierno, para informar á Don Bernardo Gutierres que las catorce víctimas habian sido despachados; un gran número de otros jóvenes expectadores y yo, presenciamos en esa mañana de memoria fatal de pie en la puerta de las casas de Gobierno, la entrada del Capitan Delgado á la sala, quitandose el sombrero ante el General Gutierres y proferir titubeando algunas palabras de mesclada vergüenza, entregandole un papel, el cual creo, que contenia la lista de los degollados, cuyos nombres doy á continuacion.

Españoles.

Manuel de Salcedo	Gobernador.
Simon de Herrera	} Coroneles
Geronimo Herrera	
Juan Echevarria	Capitan
José Mateos	}
José Goescochea	
Juan Ignacio Arrambide	} Tenientes
Gregorio Amador	
Antonio Lopes	}

Francisco Pereira Capitan.

Mexicanos.

Miguel de Arcos   Capitan

Luis hijo y *Francisco.* 2 *tenientes*

Juan Caso   Teniente.

Yo mismo he visto las ropas y alhajas ensangrentadas que esos tigres llevaban pendientes de los arzones de sus sillas, haciendo gala pública de su crímen y de haber dividido los despojos entre ellos á prorrata.

Es cierto, como he dicho, que Gutierres recibió en la propia casa de Gobierno el parte por conducto de Delgado de aquel cruel procedimiento, aunque despues desconoció haber tenido parte en la ejecucion de los prisioneros. Gutierres dice en un manuscrito, que escribió é imprimió en Monterey el 25 de Mayo de 1827 que el nunca habia dado la órden de dar muerte á aquellos catorce desdichados; pero que un gran número de ciudadanos altamente escitados é indignados contra los gobernadores españoles, indujeron á la mayoria de la junta á pasar una órden formal por lo que la guardia que los custodiaba pudiera entregarlos inmediatamente.

„La guardia añade Gutierres no podia menos que obedecer, sin esperar como debieron haberlo hecho ni consentimiento y órden para él y los prisioneros que custodiaban fueron inmediatamente sacados y conducidos al lugar donde les esperaba tan inhumana y sangrienta muerte, la que les fué dada sin autorizacion y sin los auxilios temporales y espirituales que la santa Iglesia ordena, Dios quizá, lo permitió así, en condigno castigo de las crueldades inhumanas que se habian cometido por estas malogradas personas." El que halla conocido ó pueda formarse una idea imperfecta de la clase de hombres de aquella época, aquel que pueda concebir el estremo grado de ignorancia y pasiones feroces de los hombres de esos tiempos, el que sepa, que entre los mexicanos de ese tiempo, con algunas eccepciones no habia sentimientos políticos correctos, que no conocian la importancia de las palabras Independencia y Libertad y que no comprendian las causas del levantamiento del Cura Hidalgo como como un grito de muerte y una guerra sin cuartel á los gachupines como eran llamados los españoles, admitirán y convendrán sin dificultad alguna, que una banda de los llamados patriotas, como Bernardo Gutierres, ha dicho de su motu própio „dieron muerte á esas catorce víctimas" pero la escusa es muy frívola, muy cobarde é indigna de un general, que ni debia ni podia evitar un escándalo semejante, ni menos abandonar el mando despues de ver su causa ennegrecida por una accion mas infame que la que podria autorizar á un gefe de vándalos. Consecuentemente, Gutierres participó de la atrocidad. Su disímulo, lo condenó y como Pilatos, lavóse las manos. No fué una Corte Marcial la que los sentenció como se ha publicado erroneamente.

Kemper y los auxiliares americanos se horrorizaron de hecho tan bárbaro y se preparaban salir del país, exigiendo á Gutierres lo que se les adeudaba en nombre de la República Mexicana, pero debido á las súplicas del coronel Miguel Menchaca y otros gefes mexicanos consintieron en quedarse en San Antonio, para ayudar á la causa de la independencia mexicana.

Algunos dias despues de estos sucesos se supo de certeza que el coronel Don Ignacio Elizondo, marchaba de Rio Grande hácia á San Antonio con un ejército de mas de 2000 hombres. Se puso furioso al recibir la nueva de la muerte de los Gobernadores y llegó á marchas forzadas al punto conocido por el „Alazan" á cosa de dos millas al Poniente de San Antonio.

Gutierres y Perry le encontraron allí el 3 de Junio de 1813. De las torres de la Parroquia Católica un número de jóvenes curiosos observabamos con nuestros lentes, el conflicto de las brillantes armas, y oiamos el horrisono estampido del cañon.

Elizondo despues de un combate de cuatro horas, fué derrotado y abandonó el campo dejando 400 hombres entre muertos, heridos y prisioneros. La pérdida de Gutierres consistió de veinte y dos muertos y cuarenta y dos heridos.

Entre los muertos estaba el ayudante de campo, Mr. Maricos, un jóven francés hábil, sábio, de valor person l, y tan gallardo que ni aun los mariscales del mismo Napoleon le habrian rivalizado. Apenas habian vuelto victoriosos á San Antonio, Gutierres y Perry, cuando se supo que el comandante en gefe de la Provincia, Don Joaquin de Arredondo, estaba en el Laredo en marcha sobre esta plaza, con mas de 3000 de las mejores tropas mexicanas, unidos á las fugitivas de la batalla del Alazan, quienes con su derrotado gefe el Coronel Elizondo habian incorporadoseles en el camino.—A esa hora Gutierres sin embargo de sus victorias, empezó á perder la confianza en sus oficiales y soldados. Si la bárbara y desusada conducta de Gutierres hácia los asesinados españoles, ó las maniobras políticas de Don José Alvares de Toledo, un español que habia sido mandado por las córtes de Cadiz á la isla de San Domingo, liberal y desafecto hácia el dominio del Rey de España, quien vino del Estado de la Luisiana á destituir del mando á Gutierres, operaron en el sentimiento de los Gefes Republicanos y ejército, lo que es cierto y seguro es, que su influencia disminuyó con la misma rapidéz conque habia triunfado de mil batallas. Desanimado de verse abandonado salió de Bexar con algunos de sus mas íntimos amigos para los Estados—Unidos, y algunos dias despues, el General Toledo tomó el mando del ejército; Gutierres en su manifiesto de 25 de Mayo de 1827 ha dicho que el General Alvares de Toledo solo era un fingido patriota de la Independencia Mexicana, y que cuando vino á Texas á tomar el mando de las tropas republicanas estaba en correspondencia secreta con el Rey de España, con el objeto de impedir el progreso y buen éxito de los patriotas.

Se dá como prueba de su aserto que algun tiempo despues del año de 1813 Alvares Toledo babia vuelto á España, y no solo fué recibido por Fernando VII. sino que aun fué premiado con el nombramiento de Ministro á una de las córtes Europeas. Si, es, ó no verdad, ello es un misterio oscurecido por las tinieblas del tiempo que ha trascurrido y que á lo mas prueba que habiendo sido Toledo un patriota sincero de 1813 despues tuvo la debilidad de acojerse al indulto y favor del Rey; pero si se nos permite juzgar por la reputacion y apariencias debemos confesar que las asersiones de Gutierres, están apoyadas en los epítetos que sus mismos paisanos le han arrojado á la cara. „Era político sin principios, juez sin literatura, militar sin subordinacion y cruel por esencia" por otra parte Toledo era un jóven de 32 años en apariencia liberal por principios, afluente en el hablar y de gallardo personal, de gran habilidad y maneras finas y obsequiosas. Con esta multitud de cualidades seductoras, inmediatamente captó los corazones y voluntad del ejército y los habitantes de San Antonio tomando luego como se ha dicho el mando en gefe. Por fin el General Arredondo llegó furioso é impaciente por calmar los ánimos y vengar la muerte de sus compatriotas los gobernadores. El dia 18 de Agosto y no el 13 como se ha apuntado antes, Toledo ofreció librar batalla en Medina. Este general tenia 1,500 hombres inclusos 600 voluntarios americanos.—Arredondo traia 4000 hombres. La batalla fué empeñada con gran habilidad militar por ambos partes. Los voluntarios americanos componian la infanteria y manejaban la artilleria en número de 9 piezas de 4 á 8 de calibre. La caballeria consistia de habitantes de San Antonio y vecindad y algunos individuos de Tamaulipas y Rio Grande por un movimiento estratéjico hizo Arredondo á todo su ejército levantar un grito, unánime de viva el Rey „la victoria es nuestra" y al mismo tiempo la banda dió al aire sus notas de victoria, por lo que la caballeria de los patriotas aterrorizada huyó del campo. Sin embargo la infantería flemática americana y sus artillerias sostuvieron por mas de cuatro horas, el mortífero fuego de diez y ocho piezas de grueso calibre que jugaban los de Arredondo.

Nunca pudieron sobreponerse á las imposibilidades, ni estaba en el órden natural de las cosas contender, contra una fuerza numérica desproporcionada.

La infantería americana al fin abandonó la artilleria y se largó apresurada del campo de batalla, quebrando sus rifles contra las encinas y mesquites antes que dejarlos como trofeos al enemigo, y se entregaron resueltos á su suerte. La caballeria de Arredondo les seguió con sable en mano y lanza en ristre, por largas seis millas; haciendoles terrible matanza. Asi perecieron la mayor parte de estos bravos conpatriotas. Al dia siguiente entró Arredondo en son de triunfo con sus carros cargados de heridos y moribundos. Aqui tiembla la pluma al registrar las escenas de horror que indujeran aun á los mas encarnizados enemigos de Gutierres, á perdonarle sus crueldades anteriores. Arredondo se vengó de la manera mas infame é indistintamente mandó poner presos á setecientos habitantes pacíficos de San Antonio.

Al mismo tiempo redujeron á prision trescientos infortunados en las celdas de los padres Católicos en la noche del veinte de Agosto, quienes quedaron tan oprimidos como borregas en un redil en los meses mas ardientes del verano. En la mañana del dia siguiente habian perecido 18 de ellos sofocados. Los demas fueron pasados por las armas de dia á dia, sin mas formacion de causa que una mera acusacion de ser favorecedores de la Independencia.

Por una inexplicable concidencia, parece que en San Antonio esos mismos lugares donde se perpetraron tantas crueldades fueron reservados por la providencia, y destinados para que en tiempos mas felices, vinieran á servir como instrucciones de devocion, justicia, instruccion y recreo. En donde hoy está la casa de corte, y en el frente de la balaustrada del Hotel de la Plaza principal, en una el santuario de la ley, y la otra el hospedaje que brinda lo mas delicioso que dárse pueda la gastronomia. En ese tiempo ejecuciones diarias tenian lugar y se oian á menudo los lamentos del moribundo. En donde está situada la oficina de correos, por cuyo conducto se comunican por escrito los sentimietos del alma, y se difunden el saber y la política entre el pueblo, Arredondo hizo una gran prision femenina llamada la quinta.

Allí sufrieron angustias mas de quinientas señoras casadas y solteras, cuyos esposos y padres fueron llamados insurgentes. Una guardia insolente las obligó por cuatro meses á convertir diariamente veinte y cuatro bucheles de maiz en tortillas para alimento de los oficiales y soldados de Arredondo. Allí las modestas y sensibles esposas y niñas fueron espuestas al escarnio de aquella soldadesca depravada y sufrian con frecuencia las inpuras y lacivas miradas y requiebros de oficiales y soldados que gustaban de aquel destestable y repugnante espectáculo. Doña Juana Leal de Tarin y Doña Concepcion Leal de Garza quienes aun viven en sus granjas en las márjenes de el rio de San Antonio, fueron de las del número de esas inocentes é infortunadas prisioneras de la quinta.

Aguantaron su infamante cautiverio con un valor varonil antes que ceder á las vergonzosas proposiciones de sus carceleros. Despues de la batalla de Medina, el Coronel Elizondo salió de Bexar con quinientos hombres en persecucion de los fugitivos que iban en camino para los Estados-Unidos.

En el rio de la Trinidad sobre el camino viejo de San Antonio, se alcanzó un número de hombres y familias, y allí mismo fueron fusiladas ciento cinco personas.

Tal vez se me acusará de exagerado al dar la noticia histórica de la fórmula del enjuiciamiento, por la cual esos capturados en la Trinidad, fueron condenados y ejecutados.

Elizondo tenia por Capellan á un indigno clérigo llamado el Padre Camacho cuando se aprehendian algunos de los fugitivos que llamaban insurgentes, les acarreaba al confesionario y daba órden al citado clérigo para confesarlos de conformidad con los ritos de la Iglesia Católica. Los sentimientos cristianos y de eternidad, obligaban á aquellos infortunados á confesar sin reserva la parte que habian tomado en la revolucion. El Padre Camacho en la certidumbre de estas confesiones, daba una preconcertada señal al oficial de guardia, para que condujeran á la víctima inmediatamente al lugar de la ejecucion.

Otra agravante circunstancia llenará mas de horror á los lectores. El Padre Camacho habia sido por una casualidad herido en la batalla del Alazan, por una bala fria que fracturó los muslos de su pierna. Y mas de una vez sobre el rio de la Trinidad, cuando algunos desdichados condenados á muerte pedian merced á gritos, el padre levantandose el hábito clerical, les decia. „Anda hijo y sufre tu pena en nombre de Dios, pues quizá la bala que me ha herido la haya arrojado tu fusil." Despues de estas ejecuciones en la Trinidad llevó Elizondo como prisioneras á todas las familias afligidas entre las cuales, muchas Señoras de ojos negros y hermosos, fueron obligadas á cruzar á pié maniatadas el rio de San Antonio en el mismo sitio que ahora cubre el agradable baño de Mr. Hall, é invitaba de palabra al Sexso débil á bañar sus delicadas formas. Quien habria predicho á los famosos espias del General Gutierres, Culás, Botas Negras y Ayamontes aquienes Arredondo habria hecho fusilar en San Antonio y. cuyas cabezas fueron en huacaladas y puestas en la punta de una pica en el mismo punto á donde hoy flamea orgulloso el pabellon americano en la plaza Militar. Quien habria pronosticado que treinta y tres años despues un emblema de terror se ostentaria ufano y temible para los tiranos, que una bandera que el mundo respeta habia de marcar el lugar en donde sus cabezas inanimadas fueron exhibidas? Despues de lograda la Independencia de México el Gobernador tres Palacios cruzó el rio de Medina con rumbo á Bexar, viendo las llanuras regadas de hosamenta humana, los que hizo recoger y enterrar con todos los honores militares. Me acuerdo distintamente que dejó escrito en el tronco de una encina un cuadro de madera con la siguiente inscripcion:

Aqui yacen los bravos mexicanos
Que imitando el ejemplo de Leonidas,
Sacrificaron su fortuna y vidas
Luchando sin cesar contra tiranos.

Esta es una imperfecta, pero verdadera historia de los sucesos de ese período.

San Antonio permaneció quieto y sujeto al dominio del Rey de España despues del arribo de Arredondo. El confiscó y vendió las propiedades de los patriotas que llamaban rebeldes, los que nunca recobraron, ni aun despues de consumada la Independencia Mexicana en el año de 1821.

Los nobles Ciudadanos de Bexar sacrificaron sus vidas é intereses haciendo prodigios de valor en el año de 1813. No dejaron á sus descendientes mas heredad que la indiferencia é ingratitud de la República Mexicana.

Nunca recibieron recompensa ó indemnizacion alguna y ni aun el respeto debido y gratitud de sus conciudadanos de México. Fué dado al olvido absoluto nuestro valor y heroismo por el Gobierno de la antigua y bien recordada Pátria. Por eso no creo que sorprenda á nadie el gérmen de descontento, que el pueblo de Texas abrigaba, y por cuya causa se adhiere al nuevo órden de cosas que nos brindaban las instituciones de una graude, poderosa, y agradesida República. Tal es el oríjen que dió márjen á la Independencia, de Texas, que para siempre se separó de aquel Gobierno.

Quizá mas allá pueda continuar este mismo asunto.

Octubre 30 de 1853.

Fin de los apuntes.

Selected Bibliography

Primary Sources

Anonymous. "Notes sur la premiere révolution de Texas, 1813." Jean Louis Berlandier papers, microfilm extracted from the Henry Raup Wagner Collection of Western Americana, Yale University. At University of Texas at San Antonio Library, Special Collections.

Anonymous. "Notes sur la révolution de Texas en 1813. Fournis par une femme de Béxar victime des excès des royalistes Espagnols." Jean Louis Berlandier papers, microfilm extracted from the Henry Raup Wagner Collection of Western Americana, Yale University. At University of Texas at San Antonio Library, Special Collections.

Anonymous. "To the Inhabitants of Santa Fe and Other Towns of New Mexico East of the Rio Grande" (typescript). Navarro Collection, Daughters of the Republic of Texas Library, San Antonio.

Barker, Eugene C., ed. *The Austin Papers*. Washington, D.C.: U.S. Government Printing Office, 1924-1928, 3 volumes.

Baylies, Francis. *A Narrative of Major General Wool's Campaign in Mexico, in the Years 1846, 1847 & 1848*. Albany: Little, 1851; reprint, Austin: Jenkins Publishing Co., 1975.

Béxar Archives. The Center for American History, University of Texas, Austin. These documents are indexed in *The Béxar Archives (1717-1836): A Name Guide*, ed. and comp. Adán Benavides, Jr. Austin: University of Texas Press, 1989.

Biography of José Antonio Navarro, Written by an Old Texan. With a preface by Mary Bell Hart. Houston: Telegraph Steam, 1876; reprint, [San Antonio]: Hart Graphics, 1976.

De Cordova, J. *Texas: Her Resources and Her Public Men. A Companion for J. De Cordova's New and Correct Map of the State of Texas*. Philadelphia: J. B. Lippincott, 1858.

De la Teja, Jesús F., ed. *A Revolution Remembered: The Memoirs and Selected Correspondence of Juan N. Seguín*. Austin: State House Press, 1991.

Dixon, Ford. "Cayton Erhard's Reminiscences of the Texan Santa Fe Expedition, 1841." *Southwestern Historical Quarterly* 66 (1963): 424-56, 547-68.

Driggs, Howard R. and Sarah S. King, eds. "Señor Garza Recalls Old Tio Juan." In *Rise of the Lone Star: A Story of Texas Told by its Pioneers*, 141-54. New York: Frederick A. Stokes, 1936.

_____, eds. "Señor Navarro Tells the Story of His Grandfather." In *Rise of the Lone Star: A Story of Texas Told by its Pioneers*, 267-75. New York: Frederick A. Stokes, 1936.

Falconer, Thomas. *Letters and Notes on the Texan Santa Fe Expedition, 1841-1842*. New York: Dauber & Pine, 1930.

Green, Rena Maverick, ed. *Memoirs of Mary A. Maverick*. San Antonio: Alamo Printing Co., 1921.

Gulick, Charles Adams Jr. and Katherine Elliott, eds. *The Papers of Mirabeau Buonaparte Lamar*. Austin: Von Boeckmann-Jones, 1973, 6 volumes. These papers are indexed in *Calendar of the Papers of Mirabeau Buonaparte Lamar*, ed. and comp. Michael R. Green. Austin: Texas State Library, 1982.

Hatcher, Mattie Austin, trans. "Joaquín de Arredondo's Report of the Battle of the Medina, August 18, 1813." *Quarterly of the Texas State Historical Association* 11 (January 1908): 220-36.

Ikin, Arthur. *Texas: Its History, Topography, Agriculture, Commerce, and General Statistics. To Which Is Added, a Copy of the Treaty of Commerce Entered into by the Republic of Texas and Great Britain. Designed for the Use of the British Merchant, and as a Guide to Emigrants.* London: Sherwood, Gilbert, and Piper, 1841.

Journals of the Senate of the First Legislature of the State of Texas. Clarksville: Standard Office, 1848.

Kendall, George Wilkins. *Narrative of the Texan Santa Fe Expedition, Comprising a Description of a Tour Through Texas, and Across the Great Southwestern Prairies, the Camanche [sic] and Caygua Hunting-Grounds, with an Account of the Sufferings from Want of Food, Losses from Hostile Indians, and Final Capture of the Texans, and Their March, as Prisoners, to the City of Mexico. With Illustrations and a Map.* New York: Harper and Brothers, 1844; reprint, Ann Arbor, Michigan: University Microfilms, 1966.

Kennedy, William. *Texas: The Rise, Progress, and Prospects of the Republic of Texas.* London: R. Hastings, 1841; reprint, Fort Worth: Molyneaux Craftsmen, 1925.

Menchaca, Antonio. *Memoirs.* With a foreword by Frederick C. Chabot and an introduction by James P. Newcomb. San Antonio: Yanaguana Society, 1937.

_____. "The Memoirs of Captain Menchaca" (typescript). Edited and annotated by James P. Newcomb. The Center for American History, University of Texas, Austin.

Newell, C[hester]. *History of the Revolution in Texas, Particularly of the War of 1835 & '36; Together with the Latest Geographical, Topographical, and Statistical Accounts of the Country, from the Most Authentic Sources.* New York: Wiley & Putnam, 1838.

Olmsted, Frederick Law. *A Journey Through Texas; or, A Saddle-Trip on the Southwestern Frontier: With a Statistical Appendix.* New York: Dix, Edwards & Co., 1857.

Pease, L. T. "A Geographical and Historical View of Texas; with a Detailed Account of the Texian Revolution and War." In

John M. Niles. *History of South America and Mexico; Comprising Their Discovery, Geography, Politics, Commerce, and Revolutions.* Hartford: H. Huntington, 1838.

Potter, R[euben] M. *The Texas Revolution: Distinguished Mexicans Who Took Part in the Revolution of Texas, with Glances at Its Early Events.* Reprinted from the *Magazine of American History,* October 1878. Available at The Center for American History, University of Texas, Austin.

Rodríguez, Father J. M. "Notes de Curé Dn. J. M. Rodríguez sur l'invasion des insurgés du Texas l'année 1812 et delle de 1813." Jean Louis Berlandier papers, microfilm extracted from the Henry Raup Wagner Collection of Western Americana, Yale University. At University of Texas at San Antonio Library, Special Collections.

Rodríguez, J[osé] M[aría]. *Rodríguez Memoirs of Early Texas.* San Antonio: Passing Show Printing, 1913; reprint, San Antonio: Standard, 1961.

Walker, Henry P., ed. "William McLane's Narrative of the Magee-Gutiérrez Expedition, 1812-1813." *Southwestern Historical Quarterly* 66 (1962-1963): 234-51, 457-79, 569-88.

Weeks, William F., comp. *Debates of the Texas Convention.* Houston: J. W. Cruger, 1846.

Williams, Samuel May. Correspondence. Rosenberg Library, Galveston. A calendar of this correspondence is in *Samuel May Williams, 1795-1858,* comp. Ruth G. Nichols and S. W. Lifflander. Galveston: Rosenberg Library Press, 1956.

Yoakum, H[enderson]. *History of Texas from Its First Settlement in 1685 to Its Annexation to the United States in 1846.* New York: Redfield, 1855; reprint, Austin: Steck, 1935, 2 volumes.

Secondary Sources

Alessio Robles, Vito. *Coahuila y Texas en la época colonial*. Mexico, D.F.: Editorial Cultura, 1938; reprint, Mexico: Editorial Porrua, 1978.

Almaráz, Félix D., Jr. *Tragic Cavalier: Governor Manuel Salcedo of Texas, 1808-1813*. Austin: University of Texas Press, 1971.

Barker, Eugene C. *The Life of Stephen F. Austin: Founder of Texas, 1793-1836*. Austin: University of Texas Press, 1969.

_____. "Native Latin American Contribution to the Colonization and Independence of Texas." *Southwestern Historical Quarterly* 46 (January 1943): 317-35.

Benson, Nettie Lee. "Texas' Failure to Send a Deputy to the Spanish Cortes, 1810-1812." *Southwestern Historical Quarterly* 64 (July 1960): 14-35.

Birge, M. "The Casas Revolution." M.A. thesis, University of Texas, Austin, 1911.

Broussard, Ray F. "San Antonio During the Texas Republic: A City in Transition." *Southwestern Studies* 5 (1967): 3-40

Bueno, Anastacio Jr. "In Storms of Fortune: José Antonio Navarro of Texas, 1821-1846." M.A. thesis, University of Texas, San Antonio, 1978.

Castañeda, Carlos E. *Our Catholic Heritage in Texas, 1519-1950*. Austin: Von Boeckmann-Jones, 1936-1958, volumes 6-7.

Chabot, Frederick Charles. *With the Makers of San Antonio. Genealogies of the Early Latin, Anglo-American, and German Families with Occasional Biographies, Each Group Being Prefaced with a Brief Historical Sketch and Illustrations*. San Antonio: Artes Graficas, 1937, 202-206.

_____, ed. *Texas in 1811: The Las Casas and Sambrano Revolutions*. San Antonio: Yanaguana Society, 1941.

Chipman, Donald E. *Spanish Texas, 1513-1821*. Austin: University of Texas Press, 1992.

Contreras, Roberto. "José Bernardo Gutiérrez de Lara: The Forgotten Man." M.A. thesis, Pan American University, Edin-
burg, Texas, 1975.

Crisp, James Ernest. "Anglo-Texan Attitudes Toward the Mexican,
1821-1845." Ph.D. diss., Yale University, New Haven, 1976.

Crook, Carland Elaine. "San Antonio, Texas, 1846-1861." M.A.
thesis, Rice University, Houston, 1964.

Dawson, Joseph Martin. José Antonio Navarro: Co-Creator of Texas.
Waco: Baylor University Press, 1969.

De la Teja, Jesús Francisco. "Land and Society in 18th Century San
Antonio de Béxar: A Community on New Spain's Northern
Frontier." Ph.D. diss., University of Texas, Austin, 1988.

_____, and John Wheat. "Béxar: Profile of a Tejano Community,
1820-1832." Southwestern Historical Quarterly 89 (July 1985):
7-34.

De León, Arnoldo. The Tejano Community, 1836-1900. Albuquerque: University of New Mexico Press, 1982.

_____. They Called Them Greasers: Anglo Attitudes Toward Mexicans
in Texas, 1821-1900. Austin: University of Texas Press, 1983.

Devereaux, Linda Ericson. "The Magee-Gutiérrez Expedition."
Texana 11 (1973): 52-63.

Dixon, Sam Houston. The Men Who Made Texas Free. Houston:
Texas Historical Publishing, 1924, 243-47.

Downs, Fane. "The History of Mexicans in Texas, 1820-1845."
Ph.D. diss., Texas Tech University, Lubbock, 1970.

Dysart, Jane. "Mexican Women in San Antonio, 1830-1860: The
Assimilation Process." Western Historical Quarterly 7 (October 1976): 365-75.

Faulk, Odie B. The Last Years of Spanish Texas, 1778-1821. The
Hague: Mouton, 1964.

Fritz, Naomi. "José Antonio Navarro." M.A. thesis, St. Mary's
University, San Antonio, 1941.

Garrett, Julia Kathryn. *Green Flag over Texas: A Story of the Last Years of Spain in Texas.* Dallas: Cordova, 1939; reprint, Austin: Pemberton Press, 1969.

Gibson, Dorothy Kelly. "Social Life in San Antonio, 1855-1860." M.A. thesis, University of Texas, Austin, 1937.

Haggard, J. Villasana. "The Counter-Revolution of Béxar, 1811." *Southwestern Historical Quarterly* 43 (October 1939): 222-35.

Handbook of Texas. Austin: Texas State Historical Association, 1952, 2:262-63.

Hatcher, Mattie Alice Austin. *The Opening of Texas to Foreign Settlement, 1801-1821.* Austin: University of Texas Press, 1927; reprint, Philadelphia: Porcupine, 1976.

Henderson, Harry McCorry. "The Magee-Gutiérrez Expedition." *Southwestern Historical Quarterly* 55 (July 1951): 43-61.

Henson, Margaret Swett. *Samuel May Williams: Early Texas Entrepreneur.* College Station: Texas A&M University Press, 1976.

Hinojosa, Gilberto M. "The Enduring Hispanic Faith Communities: Spanish and Texas Church Historiography." *Journal of Texas Catholic History and Culture* 1 (March 1990): 20-41.

Jarratt, Rie. *Gutiérrez de Lara, Mexican-Texan: The Story of a Creole Hero.* Austin: Creole Texana, 1949.

Jiménez, Judith M. "Joaquín Arredondo, Loyalist Officer in New Spain, 1810-1821." Ph.D. diss., University of Michigan, Ann Arbor, 1933.

Kemp, Louis Wiltz. *The Signers of the Texas Declaration of Independence.* Houston: Anson Jones Press, 1944.

Lack, Paul D. *The Texas Revolutionary Experience: A Political and Social History, 1835-1836.* College Station: Texas A&M University Press, 1992.

Loomis, Noel M. *The Texan-Santa Fe Pioneers.* Norman: University of Oklahoma Press, 1958.

Matovina, Timothy M. *Tejano Religion and Ethnicity: San Antonio, 1821-1860.* Austin: University of Texas Press, 1995.

McCaleb, Walter Flavius. "The First Period of the Gutiérrez-Magee Expedition." *Quarterly of the Texas State Historical Association* 4 (January 1901): 218-29.

McGrath, Sister Paul of the Cross. "Political Nativism in Texas, 1825-1860." Ph.D. diss., Catholic University of America, Washington, D.C., 1930.

Miller, Thomas Lloyd. "José Antonio Navarro, 1795-1871." *Journal of Mexican American History* 2 (Spring 1972): 71-89.

Milligan, James Clark. "José Bernardo Gutiérrez de Lara, Mexican Frontiersman, 1811-1841." Ph.D. diss., Texas Tech University, Lubbock, 1975.

Montejano, David. *Anglos and Mexicans in the Making of Texas, 1836-1986.* Austin: University of Texas Press, 1987.

Morey, Elizabeth May. "Attitude of the Citizens of San Fernando Toward Independence Movements in New Spain, 1811-1813." M.A. thesis, University of Texas, Austin, 1930.

Paredes, Raymund A. "The Origins of Anti-Mexican Sentiment in the United States." *New Scholar* 6 (1977): 139-65.

Peters, Robert K. "Texas: Annexation to Secession." Ph.D. diss., University of Texas, Austin, 1977.

Poyo, Gerald E. and Gilberto M. Hinojosa. "Spanish Texas and Borderlands Historiography in Transition: Implications for United States History." *Journal of American History* 75 (September 1988): 393-416.

_____, eds. *Tejano Origins in Eighteenth-Century San Antonio.* Austin: University of Texas Press, 1991.

Remy, Caroline. "Hispanic-Mexican San Antonio: 1836-1861." *Southwestern Historical Quarterly* 71 (April 1968): 564-82.

Schwarz, Ted. *Forgotten Battlefield of the First Texas Revolution: The Battle of Medina, August 18, 1813.* Edited by Robert H. Thonhoff. Austin: Eakin Press, 1985.

Tijerina, Andrés. *Tejanos and Texas under the Mexican Flag, 1821-1836.* College Station: Texas A&M University Press, 1994.

Warren, Harris Gaylord. *The Sword Was Their Passport: A History of American Filibustering in the Mexican Revolution*. Baton Rouge: Louisiana State University Press, 1943; reprint, Port Washington, New York: Kennikat, 1972.

Weber, David J. *The Mexican Frontier, 1821-1846: The American Southwest Under Mexico*. Albuquerque: University of New Mexico Press, 1982.

_____. "'Scarce more than apes.' Historical Roots of Anglo American Stereotypes of Mexicans in the Border Region." In *New Spain's Far Northern Frontier: Essays on Spain in the American West, 1540-1821*, ed. David J. Weber, 295-307. Albuquerque: University of New Mexico Press, 1979.

_____. *The Spanish Frontier in North America*. New Haven: Yale University Press, 1992.

Wheeler, Kenneth W. *To Wear a City's Crown: The Beginnings of Urban Growth in Texas, 1836-1865*. Cambridge: Harvard University Press, 1968.

Wright, Robert E. "Local Church Emergence and Mission Decline: The Historiography of the Catholic Church in the Southwest During the Spanish and Mexican Periods." *U. S. Catholic Historian* 9 (Winter/Spring 1990): 27-48.

Index